ONE MORE BREATH

A STRUGGLE FOR SELF AND SOUL

LYNETTE CHENNELL

Copyright © 2019~Lynette Chennell

Apart from any fair dealing for the purpose of private study, research, criticism or review, as permitted under the Copyright Act, no part may be reproduced by any process without permission from the author. Every effort to comply with copyright requirements has been made by seeking permission and acknowledging owners of source material used in the text.

Disclaimer:

i) This book is a collection of memories. Information gathered has come from a wide variety of sources. The personal stories and memories by individuals recorded here are their version of events and have been both provided and reproduced in good faith with no disrespect or defamation intended. Every effort has been made to ensure the researched information is correct. No liability for incorrect information or factual errors will be accepted by the author.

ii) The views and opinions expressed in this work are solely those of the author. Some names may have been changed to protect privacy however they reflect real people and events.

A catalogue record for this book is available from the National Library of Australia

ISBN: 9780648389507 paperback
ISBN: 9780648389514 ebook

Cover and interior:
Pickawoowoo Publishing Group www.pickawoowoo.com

Printing and distribution:
Lightning Source (USA, UK, AUS, EUR).

You came to me
Though my heart was closed and sore
Caught in legacy
You love me still
Holley, David and Cameron
My extraordinary angels.

Foreword

At the bottom of a rainforest lies a crystal-clear pond, framed with foliage that heightens the senses.

The magnificence of this sacred place and the illumination from the pond's surface draws an inquisitive child to its edge. She takes a deep breath and slowly bends forward to get a glimpse of her reflection.

Unlike Narcissus, she doesn't like what she sees and angrily throws a pebble directly into the centre, erasing her image. As she stares into the pond through tear-filled eyes, the child becomes mesmerised by the ripples, curious to see how far they will expand. She tosses another, then another, realising that the deeper the pebble goes the farther the ripples spread.

When Lynette Chennell asked me if I would read her manuscript and consider writing the foreword for this book, I immediately knew I would. I didn't know why I felt such a strong internal "Yes", but I have learned to respect my inner signals.

Lynette's invitation also sparked my curiosity. A seminar I led in Perth over 20 years ago, which Lynette attended, was only a vague memory. Lynette reminded me of the seminar and asked me if I remembered her because of a poem she had written and sent to me afterward. I've led countless programs throughout Australia over the past thirty years and because of this, I'm sad to say that I wouldn't even recognise Lynette if we passed in the street. For me, this is the most unsatisfying part of my work. When I travel and teach, I don't get the opportunity to share someone's journey and witness the full benefits of our work together.

I emailed Lynette back and told her I would be honoured to write the foreword. She replied saying: "Being in that seminar at that time in my life, saved my life. It is the most significant thing I have ever done, and though I had to go through more 'stuff' afterwards, the journey has been beyond anything I could have imagined. "Today, I am the woman I had it in me to be". That last line told me that it was going to be a very good read.

"One More Breath" is the story of Lynette's childhood, the negative effects of that childhood in her adult life, and how she overcame them. More importantly, she takes us on a spiritual journey where she literally breathes life back into the soul of her lost inner child and breaks the cycle of multigenerational patterns to set herself and her children free.

Lynette has given us a book that is beautifully written. Its authenticity is raw in a way that only comes across from an author who is willing to go to their inner depths and expose it on paper, so others may benefit. In doing so, Lynette Chennell has tossed a pebble in a pond that goes deep, and I believe will expand the hearts and minds of those who read it.

The 'ripple effect' of this book extends far beyond issues of surviving abusive childhoods and dysfunctional families. At the heart of Lynette's personal story is a message that will inspire the reader to overcome any unfortunate experience and show them how to make peace with the past, so they may begin living a happy and fulfilling life.

Being a psychotherapist who has worked with adults recovering from childhoods riddled with addictions, dysfunctional families, abuse and co-dependent relationships, I have been exposed to just about every horrific episode one can imagine. I have heard countless stories of victimisation and witnessed the devastating effects in peoples' adult relationships and their lives. Consequently, reading the horrific details of Lynette's childhood and subsequent adult life did not surprise me. Yet, something was different in this story.

Although exposing abuse initially gives relief, it does not effectively heal the wounds. Sadly, many never fully recover because they don't know how to turn their victimisations into victories. They go from person to person repeating their grievance stories because they don't know how to embrace their shadow, release resentment and find true forgiveness within their hearts. Lynette has done this. She becomes the teacher as she takes the reader on a journey from the darkness of despair to the optimistic options that result from opening the door of a painful childhood, to find liberation from its destructive consequences.

In the past two decades, we have been fortunate to receive great works about the Mind/Body Connection from respected specialists such as Deepak Chopra and Dr Bernie Siegal, who give further credibility to the early work of metaphysical healers such as Louise Hay. As a professional, I too take a holistic approach and believe it is important to equally address behaviours, beliefs and feelings from a spiritual perspective. I am not talking about religion, but rather principles of faith, trust, surrender, power, love, acceptance, connection, forgiveness and grace.

Professionals working in mental health, wellness and other related fields will find this book a much-needed resource to help clients identify wounds and provide encouragement to take the necessary steps to be free of them. I would also recommend this book to my clients to inspire them to find their inner voice and deepen their intuition, so they may eventually be set free from depending on others for their answers.

I often say to my clients, "take a deep breath and fear forward". Sometimes, just one more breath makes all the difference.

Shirley Smith
Psychotherapist
Author of "Set Yourself Free"

Contents

	The Dance	1
	Girl Child	3
1	Tears in the Shadows	5
2	A Different Kind of Life	24
3	Moving Right Along	39
4	Prince Charming	55
5	The Saviour of Marriage	64
6	A New Journey	82
7	The Search	97
8	Kaleidoscope	113
9	Descent to Hell	130
10	Facing the World	151
11	The Dance of Illusion	179
12	Connecting the Dots	199
13	Rewriting the Dance	217
	Epilogue	225
	Acknowledgements	226

The Dance

Each person's life is a secret unfolding, a unique dance with a rhythm and timing all its own. Nothing of the ballet is known with any surety, and while we are busy dreaming, making plans and carving our lives, life's choreographer always has the final say.

This is the story of my unfolding. It is not a tale of abuse for the sake of sorrow or blame, but a tale of love, understanding and freedom found. I seek only to give hope to others who may be lost in the wilderness.

During my childhood I suffered many forms of abuse. Compounding the physical, emotional and sexual abuse was religious abuse, as passed on to my father, and so on to me. The brand of Catholicism taught by my grandmother, as taught by those who raised her, stole the ease of breath my father needed to grow into a free man. The shadow of evil and the retribution of a punishing God eclipsed the light and creativity that was his to shine. Then he tried to take mine.

The soul-wounds of my childhood were as devastating to the adult I became, as they had been to the child who received them. My body had grown, but without much of me in it. My journey towards healing confronted me with the depth of my emptiness, my illusions, distorted self-image, self-hatred and inability to love or be loved. My experiences were a profound spiritual awakening.

What resides within me now is an enriching and abiding sense of God. Do not be mistaken. I am not referring to man's God, the God of religion. I refer to 'Life', the purposeful and all-encompassing power that drives the universe and everything within it, with a wisdom far beyond our comprehension.

With the writing of this book, I honour myself and the little girl who did not know she was beautiful, or that she was a loved and wanted expression of the Divine. My prayer is that in sharing my story I can help another find the truth of who they are.

Girl Child

The light of innocence dances bright. A girl child is born into the waiting arms of life.

Hazy swirls of colour move before new and expectant eyes; the sound of mother's soothing voice reaches her ears. Love radiates in her first tiny smile; her open heart is all she came to give.

Vulnerable tender soul, small, fragile child, feels the touch of her parents' hands upon her delicate skin. She searches their face for comfort, having left the realm of light to grow embraced by them. Delicate, gentle heart feels the first pangs of fear as hands bring a sudden sensation of pain. She cries, but mother is young, father is young, and both are busy in their troubles with each other.

Her cry is the only language she has. No words with which to speak. No way of saying, "hold me, I am afraid." Her love in all its purity knows nothing of the world. She begins to fear it is not a safe place.

Girl Child's radiance dims as darkness descends. The moon, like a spell, casts shadows.

Fragile tender spirit draws in her flowing heart, forgetting from where she came. She feels the cold, the sting of shame as her love grows crooked, fed only scraps of dying love's remains. Her parents do their best as they struggle with each other, their own tender spirits having fled with time, leaving them too lost to give.

She learns not to cry. There is no one to hold her.

LYNETTE CHENNELL

Girl child's open, flowing heart slowly breaks. Tiny cracks at first appear; little droplets of life-blood, un-noticed drain away. What used to be the sun, luminous rays of Life's warmth and magic sparkle, turns ever darker with each frightening moment, growing thorns that prick and scratch, twist and entwine, bringing a winter of forgotten dreams.

Where has the child gone?

Chapter 1

TEARS IN THE SHADOWS

I am sitting in sand underneath our silver slippery dip. There is a little girl bent over my knees with her pants down. Blindly staring ahead, sobbing through choking tears, I relentlessly smack at her bare bottom with as much force as I can muster. But my body is too small to produce the power I need to express the pain I feel inside.

Driven by overwhelming feelings of powerless rage and frustration, I try harder, harnessing every ounce of will I have as I bring my arm down, intent on hurting the flesh held prisoner beneath my hand.

My mouth hangs open as I cry in an attempt to release what I cannot speak. I feel as though my aliveness has been stolen. The little girl is sobbing too, but I cannot connect to her suffering, only my own.

This image haunts and mystifies me. What was I so disturbed and distressed about as a three-year-old, that could cause me to do such a thing, to feel that depth of misery?

Searching the archives of my mind for an answer, I hit an impenetrable wall. The harder I try to break through the wall, the larger and darker it looms, locking me out and leaving me feeling frustrated, angry and afraid.

All I have are minute scraps of odd, dreamlike images so cloudy I cannot make anything viable out of them. I vaguely recollect a blue fibro house in Adelaide, and a house in Whyalla with a dusty driveway where I once stood on a broken plonk bottle, imbedding a thick shard of glass in my foot.

I am told school life began for me in a Catholic convent when I was five years old. I recall being small and terrified in a classroom, eclipsed by towering, angry nuns in black, yelling fiercely. One of them was bringing the thin edge of a ruler down hard over my knuckles, punishment for having scraped my chair over the floor.

I was the second of four children. My brother was six months old when my mother fell pregnant with me. Another brother followed a year later and a sister three years after him, indictment of the failure of the rhythm method advocated by the Catholic Church. We were all "safe time babies", to quote my mother.

Not being able to remember myself, or recall being in a family with parents and siblings, is a strange sensation. I cannot recall myself in any solid, consistent way until around the age of six, following a move from somewhere, to a small fishing village nestled on the South Australian coast.

I have been enrolled to start Grade One, and on my first day, afraid and crying, I'm standing in front of a classroom full of strangers. The room is too big and there are too many people. I feel unprotected and exposed. I see the teacher, a very tall, wide lady with dark, almost black hair like my mother's. I think my mother is standing close by, but I cannot see her.

Our first house is built of large grey stone squares. It has light blue guttering and matching blue trim all around the windows. Behind this ordinary image a vacant mist stirs. Two deeply imprinted memories emerge like ghosts from fog.

It is early hours one morning. My younger sister is asleep on the other side of the room. I lay sleeping in my own bed and my uncle, my father's eighteen-year-old brother, lifts the covers and crawls in beside me. Facing the wall, I have my back to him. I open my eyes, woken by his touch, and see the first rays of dawn filtering in through the window, turning the dark of night into a lighter shade of grey.

I am wearing my favourite summer pyjamas. The top is a soft blue cotton shift sprinkled with tiny white flowers. It comes to just below my bottom with a frill all the way around the hem, barely covering matching bloomers. My uncle's big hands already have them down and his penis is pushing and probing at my bottom.

Petrified, I suck in my breath and go rigid with terror. Instinctively I reach down, and grab hold of my pants. I try to pull them back up, but the more I try, the more determined he is to keep them down, and the more insistently he pushes himself at my bottom. Mercifully, obscurity comes, and I go away.

It's a school day, but I have been kept home. Something has happened that requires I take a bath. I can see myself sitting in shallow water, in an old style, white ceramic bathtub. Light from the morning sun shines glaringly bright through louvre glass windows just above my head, and I can hear my mother and uncle talking out in the kitchen. Ready to get out, I call for my mother to come and dry me, but it's my uncle's voice I hear say, "It's okay Glen, I'll get it." His words strike me stiff with terror.

I watch the door with eyes like saucers, not breathing as it opens, and my uncle walks in. The next thing I know I am out on the bath mat and he is kneeling in front of me with a towel in his hands. Smiling knowingly, mouthing words I cannot hear, he prises my legs apart.

During the years of my childhood, my father was a violent alcoholic, my mother and I the victims of his rage. We both bore the brunt of his frustrations with his life and the wrath he hid from the rest of the world. I was to become the scapegoat for both my parents, someone to soak up my father's anger, and to take the heat off my mother. While he was belting me, he was not hitting her.

I don't remember my father through my early childhood, apart from one incident. It was a Guy Fawkes Night. I may have been three of four years old. The adults had built a large edifice in our back yard in the shape of a man. It had been packed with fireworks and when they went off, our yard looked to be engulfed in a huge, blazing fire. As I stood anxiously watching the sparks and flames roar against the night sky from inside the doorway of our laundry, my father, tall, lean and intimidating, strode purposefully past me. In response, my body went involuntarily rigid and my breath froze in my chest. Frightened, I prayed he hadn't noticed me. To have his attention on me was terrifying.

I don't know how old I was when he first began to strap me, but around the age of six I went to school with terrible bruises down the backs of my thighs in patterned swirls of yellow, purple and black. I distinctly remember fretting over the length of my uniform and worrying it wasn't long enough to hide what a bad kid I was.

When I was naughty it was my mother's practice to send me to my room without dinner. I'd have to wait for what seemed like an eternity for my father to come home from the pub, so he could punish me. Terror began long before he walked through the door. I would sit on the end of my bed barely breathing, mind frantically racing and overloading, knowing what was going to happen and unable to stop it. I was like a trapped animal with nowhere to go, eyes darting and searching, stricken with fear.

My father's main choice of punishment, reserved specifically for me, was to have me pull my pants down and bend over. Un-buckling his belt and sliding it out from around his waist, he'd say, "This is going to hurt me more than it's going to hurt you." He was always drunk.

My naked flesh exposed in this way was degrading and humiliating. There was nothing to shield me. I was utterly defenceless and felt a devastating sense of powerlessness over my body. The physical pain was horrendous.

When my father sent me to my room, it was always with the instruction to take my pants off and wait for him. However, there was one occasion where I wasn't given the usual directive to remove my pants. As I stood like a statue in the middle of my room, my racing mind came up with an idea to ease the pain I knew was coming. Hurriedly, I pulled my singlets from my top drawer, and layered them inside my pants to pad my bottom. When my father realised something was amiss, he made me take my pants off and discovered the singlets as they fell to the floor. My effort to protect myself and outsmart him infuriated him, fuelling his determination to make sure I suffered.

My father's belts were his usual instruments for punishment. Sometimes he used the electric cord from the frying pan, or he'd have me fetch one of my own sand shoes. Once, he took a branch from a tree, pulled all the twigs and leaves from it and used it as a switch, leaving red blood welts under my skin.

My mother must have heard my cries, just as loudly as I heard hers – shrill, piercing cries that ripped me from sleep in the middle of the night with heart-stopping terror. When all was eventually quiet, I would crawl out of bed and go in search of her, sometimes finding her half-naked on the floor, sobbing with her face buried in her hands. I would put my small arms around her and comfort her as best I could.

One night, I cautiously crept out of bed and followed the sound of my mother's screams, edging my way up the dark hallway toward the slit of light shining through the slightly open kitchen door. Peering in, I watched as my mother ran for her life around the table, chased by my father wielding a large serrated bread knife. Wearing only bra and underpants, she was desperate to keep out of his grasp, her face contorted in horror and her frantic voice begging him to stop. But he continued to lunge forward, intent on catching her. I stood stiff and hidden, breath sucked in tight, expecting at any moment to see the knife plunge deep into her body.

The bathroom came off the kitchen on the other side of the room from where I stood watching. Both my parents disappeared into it. I followed, only to find them struggling on the floor. My father was forcing my mother's back over the edge of the bathtub, holding her down with one arm across her chest. With the other, he was trying to push the hose from the old woodchip heater down her throat, at the same time wrestling with the tap, trying to turn it on.

It was obvious to the kids at school there was something wrong with me. I was withdrawn and solemn, and always alone. It was rare for me to have friends to play with, unless I was being set up for something that was going to be entertainment for them.

Acutely disconnected from the world around me, I sometimes sat alone in the lunch shed, blinded by a deluge of tears and drowning in emptiness. Once, a small group of girls found me and asked what was wrong, but I couldn't speak. There were no words, no sounds. How could I tell? What could I tell? What I held locked inside, was unutterable.

Because of the constant trauma and violence in my life, I failed dismally at school. In a continuous state of shock and traumatised dissociation, I was unable to learn. By the time I finished grade four I knew next to nothing and was held down to repeat the year again. When other kids in the class knew their times tables and how to tell the time on the clock, I wanted to disappear. I never caught up and spent one mortifying year after another struggling in the classroom. Not only was I bad and dirty, I was stupid, too.

I remember once being ill with tonsillitis and spending the day in the school sick room, floating in and out of a feverish delirium. I heard the school bell ring and children laughing, woven between long periods of frightening quiet. I kept watching the door hoping my mother would appear. I wanted her to pick me up in her arms and take me home. I couldn't understand why she didn't come. I lived in a constant state of abandonment.

When I think of my mother, I recall a solitary figure who had few friends. She was a loner and battler through her marriage, keeping our family problems concealed behind the walls of our home. I do not remember her in any meaningful way, not the sound of her voice or the warmth of her smile. The greater impression is of a distant woman with a biting anger that came out whenever she brushed my hair. She'd rip the comb through my tangles, yelling at me when I cried. I was told to put up with it. She'd had to when her mother had done it to her.

As for my father, I don't remember him ever talking with me kindly, or loving me throughout any part of my childhood. I don't remember being touched by him in a way that didn't hurt.

There were times at night when I needed to go to the toilet after being put to bed. My father would angrily accuse me of lying and say I was just trying to stay up longer. He'd follow behind wearing a threatening face, warning me if I didn't urinate I'd get a hiding.

I had no privacy sitting on the toilet and always froze with him standing in the doorway, watching over me with his hard, piercing eyes, almost disintegrating me with what felt like hatred. The light from the bulb burned bright, magnifying the size of his body as it filled in the door frame, and intensifying my awareness of how small and exposed I was.

Abuse came in many forms. One night my father and I were sitting opposite each other at the kitchen table. Drunk and in a playful mood, he said he had a trick to show me and asked if I wanted to see it. Dutifully, I said yes. He told me he could make smoke from his cigarette come out of his ears, instructing me to keep my eyes on his ears at all times. I had to watch very carefully for the smoke. Interested but wary, knowing I couldn't trust him; I fixed my eyes hard and concentrated.

As I watched intently, he took a long drag from his cigarette and sucked the smoke all the way down. His face was focused and serious. I began to think smoke really was going to come out of his ears. Then suddenly, caught completely off guard, I felt burning pain as he pressed his cigarette on the outside of my left knee. I jumped in shock, and he laughed contemptuously at my gullibility.

One afternoon, I was again in trouble for some trivial, unremembered misdemeanour, and was told the usual, "Just you wait till your father gets home." This time however, I wasn't sent to my room. For the rest of the afternoon and into the evening, I was in dread of his arrival. Later that night when he finally appeared, I held my breath and waited. I didn't have to wait long. My father called me into the kitchen. I stood looking up at him as he leaned back against the stove, staring down at me, his glare intense and threatening. I knew I was going to get it and as usual, he was drunk.

At the time, I had a loose tooth in the bottom of my mouth, right at the front. I was hoping I could delay the inevitable by telling him about it. Motioning me to come toward him, he asked if he could have a look.

Cautiously I walked forward, pleading as I went that he not touch it, it was sore. He told me not to be silly and assured me all he wanted to do was see how loose it was.

Slowly and gently, he wriggled it, just a little. Relieved, I felt my body relax, but the second I did my tooth went flying through the air, disappearing across the other side of the kitchen. My father had flicked it down so hard it had ripped right out. I stood holding my mouth in shock and pained disbelief while he laughed at the stunned look on my face.

The taste of blood made me feel sick. I thought it was over, that the cruel trick of my tooth being torn out had been my punishment. I was wrong. He still wasn't satisfied. I had to get the electric frypan cord down from its hook behind the kitchen door, pull my pants down and bend over.

Endless nights were spent in my bed huddling under the covers. The darkness moved in my room as a living entity, a swirling mass of black. Teasingly it would dance and weave as it rushed forward into my face. Then it would pull back, only to mockingly rush forward again, intent on scaring me to death. It didn't matter if my eyes were open or closed, I could still see it. There was no escape. My heart would pound erratically with so much unspeakable terror, I thought it would explode and I'd die.

Into my late teens and early adulthood, I frequently saw images in my mind of my own violent and bloody death. I constantly felt as though something was stalking me, something I couldn't see. I could not afford to stay still. Every empty room, every dark corner, it was there.

I often had trouble sleeping, afraid the devil was lurking somewhere in my room. I would hide my head under the covers and chant, "Jesus is my Saviour," over and over, as if it had the power to save my life. Eventually I would pass out from exhaustion.

It never occurred to me I had a problem relating to my childhood. I believed what I was experiencing was real. I never told a living soul how scared I was, or how I imagined I was being hunted by the devil.

In my handful of treasured family photographs, I see the likeness of a little girl I don't recognise and cannot reconcile myself as having been. She does not look like the image I have of myself. My image is faceless, tattered and dirty. The pictures I hold in my hands are in colour. The pictures in my mind are in shades of grey, as though seen through the tired eyes of an old woman, not a little girl.

The little girl in the photographs looks like the type of child who has birthdays and Christmas, holidays and laughter, sunshine and play. She is soft and sweet. Her daddy would put her on his knee and admiringly tell her she is a princess. She would have lots of friends and a pretty girl's room full of light. There would be no ghosts or dark secrets. She does not look like a child who falls asleep every night, lying rigid on her back with her legs pressed hard together, both hands cupped protectively over her vagina.

I don't remember Christmases in our home. Not Christmas carols, Christmas dinners, decorations, presents, excitement or anticipation. I only remember seeing a Christmas tree in our lounge-room once. I think I was about ten. I know we had Christmas, I just don't remember what we did.

But I do remember myself one Christmas in our local hall. It is filled with happy and excited children. Father Christmas is up on the stage calling out names individually and giving each child a present. There is brightly coloured wrapping paper scattered everywhere.

I know Father Christmas is special because he has something to do with God. Quietly sobbing and standing not far from the stage, I have my eyes fixed hard on him, silently screaming at him to please, please, just see me. I want him to hear the silent screams in my head. I want him to rescue me. Inside I am crying for help, but he cannot hear me.

No one could see I was not fully alive behind my eyes. I spent vast amounts of time absent from my body and everything around me. One day, when I was in class in Grade Six, I was sharply brought back to the awareness of my surroundings by the sound of someone calling my name. The first thing I felt was the cold, wet material of my school uniform as it clung soaked to my skin. I looked down and realised with horror I had wet my pants. When I looked up, I saw a classmate standing at the front of the room holding my lunch in the air. Everyone had their eyes fixed on me. She must have called several times with no response.

I numbly got up from my desk at the back of the class and walked to the front to receive my lunch. Once outside, I sat with my legs propped up and spread wide apart on a bench in front of me, so my uniform could dry. A group of children circled me, chanting and jeering while I stared blankly ahead, swallowing a stream of tears along with my food.

On another day, I was sliding down the slippery dip and some boys at the end of the slide were laughing. I didn't know I'd gone to school with no pants on, and they were having a great time looking up my dress. I ran home in abject horror. Like an automated robot I had no awareness of my body or what its needs were.

Sometimes I dreamt I could fly. I'd glide effortlessly above everyone. I had a power they didn't possess. I was weightless and able to move at whatever speed I wanted, fly to whatever height I wanted. From above I would taunt others with my freedom. No one could touch me. The dreams felt so real, the freedom so intoxicating and powerful, I felt the glory of my own sovereignty just enough to help make my life more bearable.

I don't know how old I was when my eldest brother began molesting me. I don't remember it having a specific beginning; like everything else it was a part of my life and something I couldn't get away from. He was only one year older than me but very much the predator, his mind corrupted by the pornographic books my father always had stashed in his bedroom.

My brother's interest in sex became an obsession at an early age. He would disappear into our parents' room while they were at work, shut the door behind him, and sit for long periods fascinated by graphic images of every kind of sex. It was inevitable he would want to try out some of what he saw. He was as much a victim of abuse as I was, himself a traumatised and neglected child, exposed to poison and the same lack of parental nurturing and guidance I was.

As I got older, I too fell prey to the lure of my father's pornography, sometimes seeking it out when my parents were not home. The pictures elicited a mixture of fascination and guilt. There are images of things imprinted on my mind as clear to me now as they were back then, some in cartoon form that would be termed adult humour, and others in glossy colour of group sex and people with animals. Seeing them at such an impressionable age, coupled with everything else going on, I internalised them in a way that distorted my perception of sex, and what it means to be sexual.

Growing up we had no boundaries, no way of knowing what was or wasn't normal. My brother saw me as an object on which to experiment and satisfy his curiosity, much like a child playing with a doll. And I'd been desensitised and programmed to understand my body was to play dirty games with, and to be used as a whipping boy for other people's anger. I had no power. My body certainly was not mine and I had no authority over it.

I remember taking a shower in one of the places we lived. The bathroom and toilet were in a separate old building at the back of the house. There were small holes in the tin walls and my brother and one of his friends were outside peering in, whispering and laughing.

Once I realised they were there my time as a free spirit, alone with the water soothing my skin, abruptly ended. I dropped my shoulders and switched to automatic. Like a well-trained seal, I began to sway and dance, really giving them something to look at. It made me feel bad, but I was doing what was expected. Games with my brother's friends became more a part of the picture as I was set up in situations for their enjoyment.

Flash images I cannot begin to articulate arise from time to time, bringing with them searing shame. They are random snapshots hidden away in a vault of secret things. When they come, I squeeze my eyes shut and contract inside, trying to wring the memories out and away from me.

My whole childhood involved sex in some form or another and it did not always come from the family. One day I went home with a girl after school to play, a rare occasion, and her father, a bus driver, was at the house working on the bus getting it ready for its next run to Adelaide. He said he had to take it out for a test drive and asked if we would like to go along for the ride. Excitedly we said yes, jumped in, and headed straight for the back of the bus.

The drive out of town was fun. We ran up and down the aisle hopping playfully from one seat to another. After being on the road for a time, the father pulled the bus over to the side of the road. There was a noise coming from the engine he said, and it shouldn't be there. Opening the doors, he asked his daughter to follow him outside to the baggage compartment. She was told to stay put and listen for any strange noises until he said it was okay to come out.

The father came back inside the bus and with a big smile walked towards me. Alarm bells began to go off in my head as my chest tightened with instinctive fear. Sitting himself down on the seat beside me, he told me he was paid by the Education Department to teach little girls like me about sex. His job was to discover if I was ready for it or not. I was scared and knew he was lying.

He then said I had to do something for him, so he would know if I was ready. I had to go right to the back of the bus, pull my pants down and feel between my legs with my fingers to see if I was wet or dry. If I was dry, it meant I wasn't ready. If I was wet, it meant I was ready.

He got up from the seat and moved to the front of the bus leaving me to carry out his instruction. Barely breathing and unable to move, I remained crouched against the back of my seat. After a few minutes he came back. With my heart pounding, I quietly told him I was dry when he asked. I knew it wasn't the answer he wanted, but he just smiled and said not to worry, everything would be okay. He knew what to do to make it wet, so I could learn about sex. He stressed if he didn't do his job, he would get into serious trouble. It was very important work he was entrusted with. Dropping my eyes to the floor of the bus, I nodded my understanding.

I was instructed to meet him at six p.m. at the gate to the cemetery, and cautioned not to be late. It was close to where I lived so I wouldn't have far to go. He would then teach me all I needed to know. Again, I nodded my understanding. He stroked my hair and told me I was a good girl.

My friend's small voice called from the baggage compartment asking if she could come out. Her father called back and gave the okay, he'd found the problem and we were ready to return to town. All the way back I felt afraid. I knew he was a bad man. Looking at my friend, I wondered if he did things to her. I felt very sad.

As soon as we got into town, I ran straight home and found my mother in the kitchen, standing at the sink washing dishes. I hesitated, watching her from a distance. She was lost in the world of her own thoughts. Wringing my hands together in front of me, I walked up to her and nervously told her what had happened. She never took her eyes away from what she was doing, did not even pause for a second to look at me, just said tersely, "Go and tell your father."

I found my dad in bed so drunk he was talking to himself incoherently and dribbling all over his pillow. Quietly I told my story again. He tried to open his eyes and lift his head from the pillow as he mumbled something inaudible. It was the one and only time I ever tried to get help from my parents. I think I was about nine years old.

There was another man somewhere in the labyrinth of my childhood. A small group of kids and I sometimes visited him at his house. He lived alone and entertained us with Charlie Chaplin movies run on his old home projector. Usually, I sat by myself and rummaged through boxes of things he'd collected over the years. My favourite box was packed with neatly folded and pressed ladies' hankies embroidered with pretty flowers and lace borders, most of which had yellowed with age.

It was said he'd been molesting some of the kids. I found out about it one day when I arrived home from school to find two people, a man and a woman, in our kitchen waiting to speak with me. My mother was there and when I walked into the room, she cast her eyes down and looked away.

One of the strangers began to speak, telling me they'd come from Adelaide to investigate the claim, and they wanted to know if the old man had done things to me, too. Frightened, I looked for my mother, but she was gone. She'd quietly left the room.

The strangers began asking all sorts of questions. Did he touch me? Did I touch him? Where did he touch me? They wanted to know everything we did, what sort of games we played and if we had pet names for our private parts. I told them he'd never touched me, and I didn't know what they were talking about.

The woman leant forward, urging me to tell the truth so they could punish the man for what he'd done. I continued to tell the truth, insisting he had never touched me. Still the woman would not listen. She said the other kids, who'd already been interviewed, had reported I'd been involved, too.

I stuck to the truth and couldn't understand what they wanted from me, or why they wouldn't believe me. I kept hoping my mother would come back into the room. I wondered where she was and why she had left me alone with these people. I felt deserted by her silent disappearance. I needed to know everything was going to be okay and that I was safe.

The strangers were becoming annoyed and threatening, saying if I didn't tell the truth and everything they wanted to know, they would take me to a doctor and have me examined to see if I was a virgin. If found to be lying I would be taken away from my family and raised in a home until I was eighteen. I had no idea what a virgin was, but it did not sound good.

I didn't know a doctor could tell if people had been doing things to your body. I was petrified. If they examined me, they would find something wrong. People had been doing things to my body for a very long time. I did not want any doctor to touch me, and I did not want to be taken away from my family. Out of my mind with terror, I made up the answers the strangers wanted to hear.

It has haunted me I may have helped put an innocent old man in jail because of my lies. I had no knowledge of whether the man was guilty or not. Over the years, I've considered maybe he had molested the other kids, in which case it didn't matter, he deserved to go to jail. But what if those people had manipulated and threatened the other kids in the same way they had done to me?

On the surface, there were some good aspects to my childhood, like spending time together as a family with my parents' friends and their kids having barbeques on the beach. Some Easters we searched among the sand dunes for hidden Easter eggs, and there were occasional weekend fishing trips on a cray or shark boat. My father had many fisherman friends.

Most people in our small town knew my parents. They were actors in the local drama club and my father wrote a lot of the productions and created many of the ideas for their shows. Both my parents had a fun and creative side, but this was the only place it could shine for either of them.

I was excited whenever the drama club put on a show. Seeing the lights and costumes brought fantasy into my life, temporarily pushing the darkness aside. It was a fleeting time of pleasurable sensation where nothing else existed. Watching my father up on the stage and seeing so many people enjoy him made me feel proud, but it was coupled with confusion over the way he shone under the lights. What I saw shining was nothing like the angry, ominous shadow that lived in our house.

Acting was something I also became involved in as a child. I usually received the lead female role in our school plays. On stage I was visible, but only as the character I played. People could not see my hollow, mechanical self or what was hidden; just as they couldn't see my father's shadow-self whenever he performed.

I also took ballet classes for a time, fantasising about becoming a beautiful and proud dancer. It gave me glimpses of hope I could be other than

I was, but they were just that, only glimpses, fleeting moments where what remained of childhood innocence was temporarily rescued.

My father was a very social man and liked to play hard, but my mother was more reserved. They both did shift work at the local hotel, my father behind the bar and my mother in the laundry, kitchen and guest rooms.

Some nights they would leave after putting us to bed, either to go to work or to socialise at the pub. But left unsupervised my older brother invented a game he called sneak-ups, where he and my younger brother would silently crawl along the floor in the dark until they reached our beds. They'd jump on us and tickle us, but it was my elder brother who always came to me, sliding his hands up underneath my blankets. The darkness amplified everything, the vastness of the night, the noise of giggling and screaming, feelings of abandonment and vulnerability, my tiredness; all I wanted to do was sleep.

My escape was the beach. Water was home to me and I swam like a fish. I spent many hours playing in the sand, fishing and crabbing off the jetty with my brothers and their friends. At those times, I seemed like any other child. I could forget the sourness of my life while surrounded by so much sunlight and wide-open space.

The only love and affection I ever remember feeling as a child was when I played with kittens. It was my one avenue for opening my heart and expressing my capacity for care and love. Sometimes I brought the odd stray home, but I was never allowed to keep it. It would be destroyed or gotten rid of in some other way.

I longed for a pet of my own. I wanted something soft and gentle to look after and nurture, cradle and keep safe. I often dreamt about finding baby kittens and hiding them in the bushes across the road from our house. I had no way of knowing it reflected my struggle to keep something delicate and fragile alive inside myself.

We did have one pet for a little while, a pink and grey Galah who lived in our back yard in a big, old green cupboard. The doors had been taken off and wire put over the front to convert it into a cage. For some reason it had a large silver meat hook inside, fixed at the top. It looked worryingly odd to me, out of place in a bird cage. But it was never a problem to the bird until someone came into our yard one day while we were all out.

Whoever it was took the bird and shoved it onto the hook, forcing the point through the soft flesh of its throat until it came all the way out of the top of its head. I found it hanging after running home from school early one afternoon after a particularly bad bout of teasing.

As I looked at the bird, huge waves of anguish twisted my stomach into painful knots. Crying, I very gently took it down, carefully lifting it up and off the hook. I took it to the house and laid it on the back steps. I wanted my mother to see it and share in my grief. We could bury it together.

I sat alone on our lounge chair staring out the front window, waiting for my mother to come home from work. The bare dirt yard outside mirrored the dry barrenness I felt on the inside, opening the floodgates to tears I could never cry for myself. I sobbed and sobbed a wracking grief that shook my body. It made my throat ache and my head hurt.

By the time my mother arrived, I'd cried myself numb and mute. I took her outside to show her the gruesome carnage, but it had disappeared from the back step, presumably taken by a stray cat for dinner.

I also remember a young black dog that picked our house to belong to. He was friendly, dopey and playful, and I so much wanted to be allowed to keep him, but he was a pest as far as my mother was concerned. She seemed to hate animals. We were told not to pat it or feed it. Doing so would only encourage the creature to stay around.

Attempts to get rid of the dog failed. He was taken down to the back shed and tied up with rope. Someone my father knew came with a rifle and shot him through the head. Blood spread in a wide circle and soaked dark red into the dirt beneath where he lay.

There was nothing about life that was pleasant or safe. Not for me and not for animals too small to protect themselves.

I don't know how life was for my siblings. I remember my younger brother being a quiet boy, lost in his own world. He played alone for hours at a time outside in the dirt, making roads with little toy cars. I think he was a gentle soul and the only one who never actively pursued me. He was not an instigator, but sometimes a hapless follower of our elder brother.

As we got older my younger sister and I played games at night, whispering ever so quietly to each other in the dark as we lay in our beds, praying our father wouldn't hear us. We created imaginary worlds in our conversations with each other. Each world had its own set of little people that lived under our blankets.

Ice Cream Land was a place where everything was made of ice cream in every conceivable flavour. When we visited, we gorged ourselves silly and complained bitterly of tummy ache afterward. Fairyland was my favourite, a magical place where mushrooms were bigger than people and flowers bloomed among great oak trees. Each tree had a small door high up in its trunk where the fairy folk lived. And Pirate Land was where we had great adventures on the high seas, looting cargo and burying treasure.

The way we said goodnight to each other at the end of our games became a ritual. We took turns in being the first to say, "Goodnight, I love you", the other following with "I love you, too". In that way we alternated who had the last word before going to sleep.

Sometimes when my sister and I bathed together, we'd touch each other and giggle, just silly, innocent curiosity. I don't remember much about her, or how we felt about each other. We were just there, in the same place, the same family, the same life with only our imaginations to hold us together.

Some nights I lay in my bed and imagined a moonbeam coming in through the window. I would climb on it and explore the universe, always knowing I could never really escape, that I would wake in the morning and my life would still be the same.

I felt no sense of connection or belonging with my family, or to my community in any way. I simply existed trapped in an intolerable nightmare.

From the moment my family and I arrived at our beach-side town, until we sold up and left to make the long trek across the Nullarbor Plain to Perth, Western Australia, my life was a series of broken moments and dark, terrifying nights. All swirls in a cauldron of memory soup.

Chapter 2

A Different Kind of Life

Perth sounded exotic to me, bringing to mind images of Persia for some silly reason. The idea of moving to such a far off and unknown place was something I couldn't comprehend, akin to moving to another planet. I had no concept of the world beyond the only place I had ever known.

During our years of living by the sea we moved house many times, going from one rental to another. We owned very little. There was nothing to complicate our leaving. We sold what furniture we had and out of the proceeds, my father bought a middle-aged, white Holden station wagon.

The roof-rack was unceremoniously stacked with suitcases full of linen and all our clothes. Mum had lined everything with plastic first, hoping to keep the notorious red dust out as we crossed the Nullarbor Plain. It did little. Everything was coated in a fine red powder by the time we reached our destination.

On the day of our departure I was riddled with anxiety and ill with vomiting and diarrhoea. I hung back in my empty bedroom, pacing the polished floorboards fearful of the unknown, mumbling my worries about how I was going to manage without a toilet. However, my mother's voice inescapably called for me to come and get in the car.

Mum had a Tupperware container full of tins of Camp Pie, bread and dry crackers resting between her feet on the floor of the car, and dad had two hundred dollars cash in his pocket. Both had to stretch as far as we could make them go. It was clear this was going to be a tight trip. All we had left in the world was now either in the car, or on top of it.

The trip across the Nullarbor was uncomfortable. We kids slept squashed and sitting up. For much of the time it was long hours of driving for my father until he needed sleep himself. In those days Mum didn't drive.

The road seemed endless. I had no idea the world was so big. For much of the way the only thing to look at was desolate, dusty land, smattered with small, dry, spindly-looking trees. Roadside petrol stops, and the odd little town in-between broke the monotony.

By the time we hit the outskirts of Perth the weight on the roof rack had slid ridiculously to one side, pulling the car over on a lean. We stopped to re-pack the load before setting off to find the man my father had organised a job with. He was to be a fisherman on a cray boat and his new boss was expecting us. Everyone was grateful to have finally arrived. We were exhausted and in need of showers.

By now the money was gone and my parents were anxious. They wondered if they'd made the right decision to embark on such a journey. There was some initial panic talk about going back, but we had nothing to go back to.

We spent our first night in Perth in a wind lashed caravan park somewhere in the city. It was the middle of winter and I could have sworn our van was going to be picked up and hurled through the air. I curled myself into a tight ball beneath my blankets, held my breath and waited for the inevitable. I was going to die for sure. I wished we'd never left our small town. At least there I was familiar with the things that threatened me.

My father's new boss gave my parents an advance of five hundred dollars; enough to initially set us up. We moved into a rented fully-furnished house directly opposite of what was to become my new school.

The house had a nice front and back yard with lawns and lots of flowering shrubs. One of the nicest things was having a fence all the way around it, partitioning off our little section of the world. My new life was alive with green and bursts of blooming colour in every direction.

In fact, the whole street had well-tended gardens with an array of plants and flowers I'd never seen before. Trees neatly lined the footpaths, each equally distanced from the other. Everything was ordered and neat, giving me a feeling of symmetry and structure for the first time.

The world I left behind was lost the moment we left the driveway of our old life. Quietly it had receded behind a veil. The dark presence that hung over me like a weighted blanket, was no more, swept away by changed surroundings. In my new life, my father was gone for weeks at a time, only coming home for short periods between fishing trips.

My new school was an unexpected shock. Going through the process of being assessed for my academic level was painfully revealing. I was confronted with just how empty of learning I was, drawing a marked difference between myself and the other children in my class. I did not fit in. Groups of girls laughed and talked in the grounds of the school during recess and lunch, and I watched longingly from a distance.

By now my breasts had developed into noticeable mounds. My mother told me it was time to go shopping for my first bra. The idea was thrilling. I'd become aware of my breasts and how they felt as they rubbed against the material of my clothes. It was a wonderful new sensation of blossoming, but my eldest brother had noticed the changes, too, and was unable to keep his hands to himself. The boys at school leered and joked among themselves, while I walked with my shoulders hunched inwards, trying to somehow make my breasts disappear.

Even though my school life was lonely and burdensome, outside of it, I experienced odd moments of lightness when alone. During the day the sun shone softly through a pane of bubbled yellow glass in our kitchen, causing rays of glowing, gold hue to stretch a shaft of light across the room. To me it was angelic light and I loved walking through it. I felt cleaner in its beam, as though the blackness was never there.

We had television for the first time and I discovered the delights of cartoons, *Bewitched* and *I Dream of Jeannie*. Friday nights mum cooked her big frypan full of chicken fried rice and we'd sit together on the lounge floor and watch *My Favourite Martian*. Money was always tight. We often had beef stew with tomato sauce during the week. Many things had changed, but the damage was done. I was already dead inside.

We moved to another house and another new school where I again sat empty-headed through half of grade seven in remedial classes, not even able to accomplish at that level.

My father must have had enough of the harsh fishing life. He'd had his share of sea boils that scarred his shins, and the demanding work that strained his back. Using his experience in hotels he took a job as a manager in a small pup in the hills, and we moved again.

I felt incredible relief to be leaving the school I was in. It was the worst experience of lonely, vacant existence of anywhere I'd been, and I was desperate to not have to go through the embarrassment of yet another new school after we relocated. In the classroom I endured enormous humiliation, each day spent wishing I could fade away. I had nightmares about it, and dreams that seemed so real where at last I was old enough to not have to go to school anymore. Each time I woke to the brutal reality and cried in my pillow.

Our new home was the pub itself. Each of us had a room originally intended for paying guests. It had been a hotel in its earlier years. We had a T.V. room of our own, and our kitchen was the hotel's main kitchen where my mother cooked the counter meals. There was also a large dining room just off the kitchen, still partially set up but no longer in use.

With my father back in our lives full-time, it didn't take long for life to become overshadowed by our history. He was still a very heavy drinker. Fighting between my parents returned with the environment and free-flowing alcohol and as time passed, my father became more and more volatile. I could feel him once again getting closer and closer to unleashing his violence on my mother. So could she.

The hotel was a rough place. Sunday sessions saw our beer garden packed with young people as bands played rock and roll. Fist fights were common. My father was the bouncer as well as the barman and was often embroiled in the fighting, banning people from coming onto the premises and receiving threats to his safety because of it.

One night, a brick came crashing through one of the front bar windows. The noise of breaking glass followed by scuffling in the hallway drew me out of our private lounge to investigate. I found my father wrestling with a man half his age on the floor. The younger man had a knife and my father was trying to take it from him. My screaming mother, heavily pregnant with a surprise addition to our family, was reaching into the fray with her hands, trying to break it up. Moments later she was shoved hard to the ground, knocking the wind right out of her. Thankfully she was unhurt, but it was terrifying to witness.

Now fourteen, my body was more fully developed. Much to my parent's disapproval, my womanly curves and well-endowed breasts were gaining me attention from the young men who drank at the hotel. They were referred to as hoodlums and I was warned to stay away from them, the beer garden area, and the main part of the hotel.

Every now and then my father would come down to our private lounge to see if I was there, once telling me he'd received an anonymous phone call from someone saying they'd seen me out in a car with a bunch of boys.

At first, I innocently enjoyed the interest I received. It began to create an awareness of something emerging from within me that was appealing. But one night after closing, my father, who was as usual very drunk, cornered me in the corridor with warnings about my safety. He pointed out my lack of strength to defend myself should someone have it in mind to rape me, and threatened to throw me to the ground there and then and rape me himself, just to prove it.

Paralysed with fear, I searched his eyes desperately trying to gauge the situation. I waited, wondering if he was going to follow through with his threat, until the sudden sound of the ice machine from the bar releasing another load into the tray, broke the frozen moment. My father went on instead to lecture me, finally letting me go after his talk ended with him in tears, telling me how much he loved me and that he was only concerned for my well-being.

I began to eat continually, stuffing food in my mouth every chance I got. It wasn't long before my curves began to disappear beneath the weight I was gaining. The heaviness I felt on the inside was becoming mirrored on my outside.

Primary school ended. I went on to high school. The alienation, failure and anguish I experienced all through the years of my early education came right along with me, only in a much larger, more overwhelming environment. Neither of my parents had ever been actively involved in any way when it came to my education. There was no interest, help or support. I'd simply been left to fend for myself. There were no discussions about life choices, future direction, work or career. No guidance of any kind.

My weight ballooned. I was now fitting into size eighteen clothes and on the receiving end of jeering and fat jokes at school. I was referred to as Fat Cat or jelly rubber, because the tops of my legs rubbed together when I walked.

I had no self-esteem or positive self-image. It didn't help having my father force me to sit next to him so he could point out the difference between my very large thighs as they spread over the couch, and his alcoholic, stick-skinny ones. He told me he wanted a daughter he could be proud of.

I began to reflect on the hope that something other than the world I lived in existed. When I hoped hard enough I could almost feel it. It was there, just beyond the veil of my unhappiness, but I couldn't touch it. Looking at the night sky gave me comfort in a strange way. I started writing down my thoughts, putting words to my heartfelt longings on paper.

I longed to know about love and the beautiful things of life. I used to drift into the ironing room where an old lady my mother employed, stood for hours doing our laundry. I'd talk to her while gazing out the window with a distant stare, and ask about love, what it was and what it felt like. There had to be more to life than what I knew, otherwise what would be the point. But I had no idea what it was.

For my mother, all the hard work, fighting, arguing and undercurrent of threat coupled with the late stages of pregnancy, eventually took their toll. I came home from school one afternoon to find her lying on our lounge in front of the television, almost unconscious, sobbing and incoherent. I realized something was terribly wrong when she began gagging and coughing so hard it seemed she was choking. Her large pregnant belly tightened into a rigid ball each time she doubled up with the force of her coughs.

I tried to sit my mother up, but her arms began flailing in front of me, trying to push me away. All she could say was, "I want to die. Just let me die." Rambling and unable to open her eyes, her hand clumsily searched the floor for the bottle that contained her remaining pills; pleading with me to give her what was left. She'd taken an overdose of Valium.

Hysterical, I ran towards the front bar calling for my father. When I told him what my mother had done he simply laughed with contempt. He said she was a stupid bitch and not to worry about it, just leave her be. Horrified, I pleaded with him to call an ambulance, but he just continued to laugh. As usual, he was drunk.

Hatred rose in me for the first time. I looked at my father with disgust and through clenched teeth, spitting the words with spite, I told him I hated him before running off. What happened next, or who called the ambulance, I couldn't say.

But our local ambulance did come. I remember the man who arrived with it. He was familiar. He knew my parents and was from our town. I can see him standing in the hotel's hallway, just near my parents' bedroom. The space in and around the memory is clouded with greyish, murky shadow. I don't know if it's because the hotel is closed and the main lights turned off. It's as though I'm viewing the scene through a tunnel, separated by time and distance. He's been to see her, and I think she's been put to bed. It's late and he's talking to someone. The atmosphere is serious and hush hush.

I worried my mother's attempt at suicide was going to affect the baby. I felt the weight of the concern and fear my father should have carried. Someone had to care. Thankfully my little sister was born without any apparent harm, but while my mother was in hospital, my father played and strayed.

On the second morning following the birth, I woke to find two strange women, messed up hair and eyes smudged with makeup, prancing about our kitchen in tee-shirt and underpants. It was obvious there'd been one hell of a party. I had the feeling they'd been with my father, and as I uncomfortably went about preparing myself for school, they helped themselves to whatever they wanted.

My father was conspicuously absent. He wasn't in the main part of the hotel or the bedroom he shared with my mother. It occurred to me he was sleeping off his drunkenness in one of the guest rooms, but as soon as I had the thought, it quietly retreated along with my awareness of that part of the hotel. It was too much for me to deal with.

It was obvious to my elder brother the hotel wouldn't open without our father to prepare for opening time. Worried, he decided to stay home from school and take care of it himself. I stayed to help. We knew well enough how to set up a bar and run off the taps.

Thankfully a staff member arrived on time for the morning shift, releasing us from our anxiety and burden. The rest of the day was ours. While my father lay comatose somewhere, my brother took the keys to our battered station wagon and we went joy riding out of town. No one ever knew.

When my mother came home, there was no welcoming family introductions. My new baby sister simply appeared in a bassinet ensconced in the quiet of the dining room. Without warning I came upon her heading to the kitchen after arriving home from school. Startled, I initially kept my distance, trying to comprehend how she was going to fit in. It took a while before I could bring myself to go close. Looking into her bassinet, I was awed by how small she was. Slowly, I reached out and touched her. It was strange to have such a big change in our family. Her presence puzzled me, but life went on regardless.

We had been at the hotel for well over a year and it was time to take our first holiday. The owner of the business was to run it in my parent's absence. We spent six weeks by the sea in a small town my father had stayed at during his cray fishing days. We played in the sand, fished off the jetty and generally lounged around, with no inkling of what was waiting for us when we returned.

It was close to lunch time. My mother and father disappeared into the hotel, presumably to check in and see how things had been going while they were away. My brothers, sister, and I ran to our rooms, grateful to be home and among our own things again.

After settling in I headed towards the kitchen, but the dining room door was locked. No one seemed to be around, and the hotel was eerily quiet. I went around the back to another door, and found my mother standing by the kitchen table, shaking uncontrollably. I asked her what was wrong, but she couldn't seem to reply. When I asked again, she managed to say that two detectives had taken my father into the dining room. They'd been waiting for his return and he was in serious trouble.

While we were away on holiday, the hotel's owner had taken the opportunity to go through the books, and he'd found a three-thousand-dollar discrepancy. On paper the figures just didn't add up. He'd called the police and laid charges of embezzlement against my father.

During the long hours the detectives had my father in the dining room, they accused him of stealing the money so he could run off with our old cleaning lady, asserting they were secret lovers. My father had bought the woman a silver cigarette lighter with her name engraved on it for her last birthday, and the detectives used the fact to fabricate an accusation. It was one of many scare tactics designed to harass and bully my father until he was out of his mind with worry.

No one was allowed to speak to him or see him. In the time they had him alone, they convinced him his only chance of staying out of prison was to plead guilty. It was a first-time offence and the court would take that into consideration, but if he continued to deny his guilt, even if he was innocent, it would go badly for him. Trusting, in shock and unable to think straight, and with no legal representation or opportunity to even speak to a lawyer, my father acted on the cajoling advice of the detectives.

A court case ensued, and my father never stood a chance. He was sent to jail for eighteen months with a minimum of nine months to serve.

Unquestionably, my father was not a good husband or a good parent, but he was not a thief. His crime was one of alcoholic negligence. He had not kept the books up to date and was unaware a staff member was pilfering stock, mostly bottles of Gin. He was also unaware my elder brother and I had been stealing cigarettes and small amounts of change from the cigarette till; never dreaming what was going to eventuate. We sold the smokes at school for five cents each and spent the money at the school canteen.

Suddenly we had no father and my mother was left to pick up the pieces alone. Our lives were completely shattered. We had to leave the hotel and find somewhere to else live. A friend located a house in the same town. Once settled, my mother was lucky enough to get a job at a resort complex not far away. She had to take a crash course in driving to be able to get herself to and from work.

Given our situation, I was taken out of school mid-way through second year to become surrogate mother in the home. It was the only solution to our crisis. I was now fifteen and failing anyway, so my parents weren't bothered about interrupting my education. Even though the circumstances of my leaving were less than desirable, I was grateful that my torturous school life was finally at an end.

Mum's hours were in blocks of shift work. She was gone a lot of the time and frequently at night. I cooked and cleaned, watched my little sister as she learned to walk, and felt confused and sad when she called me mummy. I made chocolate cake with chocolate frosting sprinkled with nuts for the kids to take to school for recess, and I burned dinner often. Mum used to joke about always having to buy new saucepans.

Sometimes late at night I sat on the back steps of our house looking up at the stars, wondering where I'd come from. I felt abandoned by something I couldn't remember but longed to be reunited with, and wondered if I'd been delivered into my family from some distant planet far away. Inside I nursed a hurt I could not even begin to understand or express.

One day while my mother was at work, I snuck into her room and swallowed some of her Valium. I wanted to escape the weight of my life, the insecurity, fear and confusion. But feelings of guilt over leaving my mother with no one to help her while dad was gone had me rushing to the toilet. I put my fingers down my throat and vomited up the pills, then sat on the cold cement floor of the outhouse and cried. We moved house a few more times, going deeper into the hills and closer to my mother's place of work.

Throughout the years I'd continued to be on the receiving end of my brother's sexual curiosity, but it abruptly ended when he joined the Navy at sixteen. The first time he came home on leave after a considerable absence, he was like a different person, a stranger. He didn't seem interested in me and he didn't touch me anymore. Oddly, I felt rejected. I struggled with the changes and the emptiness.

I don't remember how it started or who initiated it, but soon after, my middle sister and I had a sexual experience together. I'm imagining it came out of some kind of automatic gravitation, a turning towards each other in an attempt to feel less ignored and alone. It had never happened before.

I can see her standing in my door way asking if I wanted to do it again, and as I looked at her, I had a jarring moment of clarity. Standing before me was a young, vulnerable girl, lonely, and smaller than me. In that moment, I realised that as the older sister; I was now the one in the position of power. Gently, I told her what had happened couldn't ever happen again. It was wrong, and I didn't want her to be hurt that way.

The sexual exploitation was over. My body let go all the tension it had been carrying, and I felt enormous relief.

My father qualified for work release after he was moved from the maximum-security prison in the city, to a low security facility in the hills. My mother was able to secure him a job as a barman at the Resort where she worked, and after his full release, he stayed on to become the bar manager. Later, he managed the restaurant.

I have no idea how I managed to look after my baby sister. I can't remember much of what I did or the time we spent together. Time had no meaning. My weight ballooned still further. I was now fitting into size twenty-four clothes. Eating was the only thing that bought me any gratification. I soothed myself through the pleasures of oral flavours and textures. Everywhere else I was numb.

After dad came home from prison, I still filled in for my parents while they both did shift work trying to get us back on our feet. From then on I received five dollars a week, and not long after that, a gift.

I was full of excitement and anticipation as the huge box was brought into the room. I never received presents. When I looked in and saw a red vacuum cleaner, I was shattered. I didn't want to disappoint my mother by appearing ungrateful, so I took it out, plugged it in and happily got to work.

When I was sixteen my parents arranged for me to do some casual work in the supermarket/cafe section of the Resort. I loved the involvement with people and the accomplished busyness of serving and clearing tables. My hours fitted with their schedules and my duties at home, and with all the activity, I began to lose a little weight. Later, I was moved across to the kitchen of the restaurant my father managed, starting out as a general kitchen hand.

I was put to work doing dishes alongside a much older man. Right from the start he flirtatiously lavished me with his attentions. At the time, I never noticed the age difference; I was too busy enjoying being noticed. Starved for attention, it made me feel alive. Within a short period of time he gained my trust and became a friend. He also won over my mother with his smile and friendly, attentive conversation.

We began a sexual relationship after some sweet-talk and coaxing. When it came to my body, the needs of others came first. Unable to say no I told him I was scared of getting pregnant, a naïve attempt on my part to hold him back. But he assured me it was perfectly safe, he'd had a vasectomy years ago. It never crossed my mind he'd lie about it. In high school, I'd heard of a couple of girls trying to trap boys by getting pregnant, but I never imagined a grown man would want to do it to a girl.

The weeks passed with us secretly having sex. I hated it. It was uncomfortable and made me feel dirty, but it kept him happy. I was afraid of losing the attention of the only person who showed any interest in me.

One morning I woke startled and covered in sweat as the awareness hit me that I was very pregnant. I sat bolt upright in total disbelief, not understanding how I knew. I hadn't had a single thought about it. Shocked by the realisation, I was overcome with horror, yet at the same time I was also aware of an odd feeling of not being alone. It was strangely comforting; in the same way it's comforting to have someone silently hold your hand while you struggle to digest unexpected information. There is nothing they can do for you other than just be there.

I told my mother that same morning and begged her to be the one to tell my father. I couldn't face him. She refused, saying it was my mess, my responsibility.

I waited alone that night for my father to come home from work. The house felt stark and empty. When he eventually arrived it was nearly midnight, and as usual, he was drunk. Nervously I told him I needed to speak with him, and as we sat down on the couch together, I thought I saw a look of concern flash across his face, briefly giving me the courage I needed to blurt out my news.

Tears filled my father's eyes. He put an arm around my shoulder and reassuringly told me not to worry, everything would be alright. Held in that moment, I experienced connection and safety for the first time in my father's arms.

It was the last time he and I ever spoke of it, and the last time I ever saw his softness. The next morning those feelings of closeness and safety were gone. Everything was as it had always been.

My mother took over. She'd already decided how things were to be handled. Through a friend, she found a doctor who performed terminations. The pregnancy was confirmed and from there, the details arranged. I had no say in the matter. My mother was not prepared to be a grandmother, and that was that.

I loathed my baby's father for lying to me about being unable to have children. It was easy to unleash on him my angry powerlessness over what was happening to me. When I confronted him with the news I was pregnant, vindictively telling him I couldn't wait to get rid of it, he looked stunned that I'd had the courage to tell my parents. He'd expected I'd run away with him rather than face them.

As my body changed, I became aware of intense feelings of love and wonderment flooding through me. My belly was beginning to round out and my breasts were swollen and tender. I could sense the life inside. How this baby came to be didn't matter. I wanted to keep my child, cautiously raising the possibility with my mother. Horrified and angry at the suggestion, I was abruptly told not to think such ridiculous thoughts. Her reaction was like a sharp slap in the face. As always, I squashed my feelings down. My body was not my body, not even the child I was carrying was mine.

I was three months pregnant when I had the abortion. I had to endure the disapproval and judgmental disdain of the doctor who performed the procedure and the nursing staff who tended me. When it was over my father picked me up from the hospital and took me home. I sat in the car quietly clutching my cramping stomach in a silence that echoed the desolation I felt. Not a word was spoken. All I could hear were the sounds of my own voiceless screams. I wanted to cry, but there was no point.

When I got home, no one asked how I was or if I needed anything. Everyone went about their usual business and I was expected to do the same. As the day wore on the cramps became too much. I asked my mother for something to relieve the pain but was tersely told to put up with it. What I really wanted was some kind of contact, or at the very least some acknowledgement of my needs, but she wouldn't even look at me.

I felt weird and unreal. My baby had just been sucked from my belly and I ached with unexpressed grief. I wanted to scream, but all I could do was go silently along with the denial it had ever happened.

The whole day was crazy-making. My only source of comfort was the brand new, floor length, bright yellow quilted dressing gown my mother had bought me for my hospital stay. I wore it buttoned through from my neck to the floor. It was the only thing I had that provided me with a reassuring sense of being held together.

Chapter 3

MOVING RIGHT ALONG

My parents decided they needed a fresh start and change of scenery after all their troubles. They took a job in a small eastern wheatbelt town as managers of the local bowling club. Nearing eighteen, I was suddenly relieved of my home duties and free to get a fulltime job of my own. But I had no skills, little education and opportunities for employment in the town were scarce.

The town's hotel was my only hope and thankfully, I managed to secure a position as a housemaid. Eventually I took extra shifts in the kitchen, but once I turned eighteen, I was unceremoniously pushed behind the bar. It seemed inevitable. Initially I was terribly nervous and felt the scrutiny of everyone's eyes. Yet to my surprise, once I got over being shy and uneasy I enjoyed the work, especially on a weekend night. It filled a friendless void.

I felt exhilarated at being able to run a busy bar packed with customers on my own, and felt proud of my ability to keep every glass full under pressure. I developed a smiling and affable persona and loved the compliments and attention I received. There was a safety about having the bar separating me from the men. I could be sweet and flirt, and they could look but not touch. I worked hard, lost more weight, and was befriended by one of the local girls. We shared the same first name, and before long, we were inseparable.

Along with my new friend came the opportunity to socialise. I was introduced to everyone she knew. It was confusing and disconcerting to watch them all together. They were very close and comfortable in each other's company. They sat on each other's' laps, getting up and moving around freely whenever it suited. There was lots of laughter and touching, a hand resting here, an arm draping a shoulder there, and random hugs on the way past to move to the next lap, the next opportunity for catching up and conversation. If anyone touched me, I froze. I was all locked up inside.

On one of my nights off, my friend and I joined a gathering of other young people in the lounge bar. It was the usual weekend crowd consisting of just about everyone of age in the farming district. Drinking beer and listening to blaring music on the juke box, I looked over to a table on the other side of the room and almost fell into a pair of large, sparkling brown eyes looking back at me. The young man and I smiled at each other. He was extremely good looking, tall and muscular with wavy, jet black hair. My friend told me he lived locally and was a shearer.

I was invited to sit next to him at his table and by the end of the evening, we'd arranged a date to go to the drive-in movies. The last thing he said to me before I left to go home was, "Have you noticed the difference between your arm and mine?" Frowning, I looked down at our arms as he placed them alongside each other on the table top. His was black and mine was white. I hadn't even noticed.

We became an instant item and the new focus for small town gossip. I didn't care. I was smitten and for the first time experiencing my body respond sexually to kissing and touching. It was a surprising expression of how light and fluttery my heart felt. But when it came to actually having sex, it was awkward and uneasy. I had no idea what to do other than just lie there, which had been the only requirement when I was a child.

My parents were uncomfortable and embarrassed by my involvement with an Aboriginal. Their immediate response was to try to shame me into not having anything more to do with him. I was shocked and incensed by their attitude.

Once a bit more information about my boyfriend's family emerged, exposed enthusiastically by concerned locals, their protests increased. Apparently they had a bad reputation for drinking and fighting and were often involved in street brawling, particularly his father and an older, more violent brother who lived with his girlfriend in a neighbouring town.

Unfazed, I continued to defend my boyfriend. He didn't seem out of the ordinary to me. Wanting to make my own way and control my choices without interference, I took a room in the town's only boarding lodge. It had twelve good-sized rooms for tenants, a large communal kitchen, lounge, laundry and separate male and female bathrooms. One of the best things about it was for the most part, I was the only occupant.

My boyfriend and I became engaged and we had our engagement party at the lodge. His family and mine attended, but both sets of parents only endured the celebration. Neither group felt comfortable with the other.

My fiancé enjoyed drinking, but then so did everyone else. It was how people had fun. He also had a moody side. I unwittingly seemed to do things that somehow, I was supposed to know not to do. Each upset was a shock and they would come out of nowhere. I'd try to understand what it was I'd done, then apologise and plead for forgiveness so he'd smile at me again. Losing his approval brought on a terrible, panic filled pain.

I couldn't get comfortable in our relationship. It was way too unpredictable. I became nervous and watchful, needing to hold myself taut and ready. Intrusive, scary thoughts, together with grotesque images of my own dead and bloodied body, started popping into my mind.

The local shire decided to close the lodge and I moved back home with my parents. I couldn't hide the difficulties in my relationship. I was told I could do better, which was puzzling to me. Everything they said about my fiancé, and his family, was in many ways true about my own. To my mind the only difference was our troubles were hidden behind an acceptable front, while theirs were sprawled out in the open.

It was impossible to believe I was worth anything more than the way my own parents treated me, and each other. It seemed hypocritical to be told I was lowering myself and embarrassing them, when at the same time rumours were rife about my father and a well-known female member of the bowling club. His own alcoholism was in full swing, coupled with the same ugly behaviour he'd always bestowed on us behind closed doors.

My father's double standards and my mother's frequent barbs about me becoming just like a 'black woman', were hurtful and only served to make me more determined to stay in the relationship. My mother kicked me out of home and I moved in with my fiancé and his family, where I saw the same abuse of alcohol and family dysfunction I'd grown up with, just in another culture. I ended up out of my depth and mixed up with racial tension in the town, becoming identified as one of them by association.

On the surface I was accepted, but there was an undercurrent of contempt from the females in my fiancés family. I was white and an outsider. I was terribly out of place and uncomfortable. Cockroaches crawled into and over everything at night, including me as I slept, and everything most families took for granted as essentials in the home, were often missing. Some evenings were spent seated around the kitchen table, where I heard scary stories about secret happenings and the magic of the Aboriginal Kurdaitcha Man, stirring up familiar dark worries from childhood.

One such night, I was introduced to a Featherfoot who'd come to visit from up north. He was tall and wiry with skin like shiny black opal. I was so filled with fear of him, that when his intense brown eyes met mine, I felt pierced by his stare, like I had no power to keep him from penetrating every part of me. His glare seemed to crumble my insides, obliterating whatever internal boundaries I had, safeguarding my precarious inner world.

I caught pubic lice. My fiancé told me they must have originated with the girlfriend he'd had before me. I was ignorant about sexually transmitted diseases, but it left questions in my mind about his trustworthiness and fidelity. We had a fight and I moved back home. I received the appropriate treatment and got rid of the lice, but the stigma of where I'd been and what I'd caught couldn't so easily be cleaned away. My mother sterilised everything and wouldn't let me use anything in the bathroom that might be touched by someone else in the family. I was dirty and diseased. The way she looked at me made me feel stained.

I tried to break up with my fiancé, but he'd ring our house and fiercely manipulate me into staying with him through threats against my family. He told me he would kill both my parents.

During one of those calls, my father stood nearby listening to my end of the conversation, watching the struggle I was in. I could sense his preparedness to do battle to help get me free. All I had to do was say the word, but I never did. I was already caught in a numbing struggle, somewhere between the searing hold of painful ownership, odd moments of illusory first love, and the powerlessness of low self-esteem.

Most of the time I felt lost and alienated. I most keenly felt it one day while on an out-of-town shopping trip with my mother. We'd called into a coffee shop for lunch before heading home, and were seated next to a table of four young girls around my age. They were chatting and laughing happily amongst themselves. I studied them intently, watching every smile, every gesture of delight they expressed in being together. I couldn't keep my eyes off them. I wanted to be like them and wondered at being part of that kind of belonging. The girls caught me staring and began to laugh and whisper. It was stinging to be snickered at.

My fiancé moved into the town's single men's quarters, a dilapidated old wooden dwelling once used for transient shearers. I moved into his small room with him and got busy fixing it up in the hopes of making it look less destitute and rundown. I cleaned and put a floral-patterned contact on the panels of the old wardrobe and bedside table top.

However, it wasn't long before my fiancé's explosive and aggressive behaviour drove me back to my parents' house, taking with me two budgies he'd bought for me while on an outing to a wildlife park. I wasn't allowed to have them inside, my mother said they were messy and carried disease. I placed them outside, high up on top of an old wardrobe out of reach of my sister's cat. He was the only animal to make it as part of our family, and I felt the hurt of what I saw as my sister's favouritism.

Weeks passed in oblivion before I remembered I had birds. I ran to the cage and reached for it holding my breath, knowing they must be dead. The shock was brutal. They'd starved to death in the cage, eating every scrap of empty shell from spent seed, as well as their own droppings, before dying. I cried with shameful sorrow and added it to the already extensive list of things about me that were unforgivable.

While my 'on again off again' relationship raged, I moved randomly between my parents' house and anywhere else I could stay. Somewhere along the line, I became very ill and had to take a week off work. I was so sick I could barely get out of bed. I had a high fever, chronic pelvic pain, and a profuse vaginal discharge of thick, yellowish mucus, mixed with fresh blood. Embarrassed and unsure of what was wrong, I went to the doctor without telling anyone of my symptoms. He never told me what I had, but put me on a long course of very strong antibiotics. My fiancé had to go on them too.

During one of our break-up periods, I moved to the city for a few weeks with the older sister of a casual friend. She was an unmarried mother with two young children and while we got on well, it wasn't my life and I felt cold, lonely and adrift. My fiancé found out where I was and came looking for me, sweet talking me back with promises of love and change. It didn't even last the three-hour drive back to the wheatbelt.

Once at the single men's quarters, my fiancé opened the door to his solitary room with its curtain-less louvered window, scuffed and faded wooden floorboards and functional, prison style metal cot, and I crumpled inside. I wanted to be somewhere else, anywhere else but here, facing this desolate life. He patted me on the shoulder, nudged me forward and said everything was going to be alright.

My nineteenth birthday came on a Saturday. It was the middle of the afternoon when I found my fiancé sitting in the front bar of the hotel drinking with his friends. I'd been hoping he might do something nice for me. When I reminded him it was my birthday, he took twenty-five dollars off the bar and threw it at me. My heart plummeted, but I took the money and bought myself a pretty bracelet, telling myself it had come from him.

Spring came bringing a dishevelled circus to town with a litter of unwanted puppies. I was easily persuaded to take one, and chose the runt of the litter, a bedraggled, wide-eyed little girl I named Mitzy. She became my closest companion and as she grew, she followed me everywhere.

My parents left to go on holiday back to South Australia. Suddenly I felt incredibly vulnerable by their absence. The mistreatment I received from my fiancé was worsening, and one night as we lay in bed I tried to get him to understand how the way he treated me, made me feel. His response was to put his feet in the middle of my back and viciously shove me out of the bed and onto the floor.

I went from being shoved to being slapped, from being slapped to being jabbed in the jaw with just enough force to cause humiliation and pain, but no noticeable bruising. If any man looked my way whenever we were out, I was accused of being a slut and punished. I was told I wasn't worth marrying and no one would ever want me.

Afraid and desperate to shield myself, I ran to my parents' house, hoping somehow a window or door had been left unlocked. Peeking through all the keyholes, wishing I was on the other side, I came across a key left in on the other side of the laundry door. I couldn't believe my luck.

Hurriedly, I looked around and found an old sheet of newspaper to slide under the door, then a stick to poke the key out, praying it would land on the paper when it fell. Thankfully it did. After carefully withdrawing the key, I gratefully let myself inside and locked the door behind me.

When my parents returned it wasn't easy to persuade my mother to allow my dog to stay. I begged and used every conceivable argument I could think of, including the fact my sister had the cat. In the end, she felt cornered and gave in, on the condition the dog was never to come inside.

One weekend I went to the city with a couple of friends for two days, and asked my mother if she would look after Mitzy while I was gone. I was a little nervous about it, but all she had to do was feed her and keep her in the yard. As soon as I got back, I called for her. I'd missed her terribly and knew she would have missed me just as much. But she didn't come.

While I was gone, a man who lived nearby had run Mitzy over on the road just outside our house. He'd known she was my dog and had deliberately run her over. She'd survived the accident but had been very badly injured. A policeman was called to come and shoot her. Mum said while everyone stood around watching, Mitzy had lifted her head, and with tears in her eyes, seemed desperately to be searching for me.

Grief-stricken, I cried for weeks, unable to cope with her loss. Her death became another cross I had to bear. I constantly went over in my mind the times I'd forgotten to feed her, the times I'd snuck off so she couldn't follow me, and worst of all, I hadn't been there for her when she died.

I lost my job at the hotel. There'd been a change of ownership and the new people had their own staff. There was no opportunity for employment anywhere else, so I was forced to look for work outside the town, and managed to get a housemaid position in another hotel, miles away.

I hadn't been gone long when I received a phone call from my mother. My fiancé had apparently let himself into their home in the middle of the night and had crawled into bed with my fifteen-year-old sister. Gutted beyond comprehension, I quit my job and rushed right home, hoping to find it had all been a terrible mistake.

I remember being in the courtroom. I was standing beside him, bewildered and uncertain of what to feel or believe. Apparently he'd been very drunk on the night in question, and there was talk maybe drugs had been involved. In any case he'd been completely off his head, unable to explain his actions or remember much of anything, only that he hadn't meant any harm.

In my mind, I grappled to come up with my own explanation, something I could understand. Maybe he'd missed me and in his drunken state forgot I wasn't at home. Maybe it had been me he was looking for, only he went to the wrong room.

It was an agonizing drama and it drained from my memory, just as all other horrifying things did. I can't even remember leaving the courthouse or what the outcome was. Perhaps he received a fine, or possibly only a warning as a first-time offender. I have no idea.

From then on he came and went from town like an elusive shadow. Knowing he had to go up our street to get to his place, I would lay in bed at night in my parents' house with my heart breaking and ears straining towards the road, hoping to hear the sound of his car drive past. The ache was almost too much to bear. My sense of identity had become so non-existent it felt as though I could only breathe if I had him to breathe through. I was so used to being an item of property, that now I was without an owner, I was lost in the wastelands.

For a while I occasionally bumped into him at the hotel or attending the same party on a weekend. I would try to get him to want to be with me the only way I knew how, by throwing my body at him. But all I got for my troubles was more degradation, humiliation and violence.

I began to go off the rails.

Going to gravel pit parties held in bushland out of the town became a common thing. Car loads of young people congregated and everyone's cars were parked in a wide circle, headlights pointing centre. Wood was gathered and large bonfires lit, illuminating frantic, wild, alcohol induced play. I danced, drank and fooled-around, both laughing at and trying to get away from my worthlessness, anguish and inner pain.

My elder brother came to visit while on leave from the Navy after a long absence. The house was abuzz with excitement at his impending arrival. Everyone was so proud. My dad had nick-named him 'The Admiral'. I was particularly in awe. He'd grown into a worldly man with an aura of travelled mystery, and he looked wonderfully impressive in his naval uniform. Timed to coincide with his visit, my uncle also came for a holiday.

Not long after their arrival, I was invited to what promised to be a big event party in an old farm house a few miles out of town. I was excited to be able to invite my big brother along so I could share my turf with him and show him off. My uncle came, too. Both men saw it as an opportunity to check out what the town had to offer in terms of local female talent.

There were people everywhere and music rumbled loudly through the house. Alcohol flowed abundantly, and it wasn't long before I was as smashed as everyone else. With all that had been going on in my life, I needed no encouragement. I was hell-bent on having a good time.

Having my brother and uncle around seemed to make me feel even more edgy, restless and out of control. I played up my sexuality, dancing and laughing from room to room. I ended up in a bedroom half-naked and having drunken sex with some guy I don't remember. After it was over, I re-joined the party, not caring about anything except getting another drink.

Walking into the lounge I noticed my uncle sitting on a chair to the side of the room. I hadn't seen him for many years, and up until that moment, I hadn't felt anything but my well-practiced state of disconnected indifference to his presence. What he'd done to me as a six-year-old was hidden and of no consequence to anyone. But suddenly, it was there, this unspoken secret only he and I knew.

Flirtatiously, I sidled over and sat on his lap, putting one arm around his neck, deliberately being provocative. His discomfort was obvious, and I wondered if it was only because we were in public. Drawing myself close, I put my mouth to his ear and whispered bitterly, "What's the matter; don't you want me now that I'm not a little girl anymore."

Abruptly, my uncle pushed me off his lap and stood up, indignantly telling me he would never forgive me for what I'd just said. Mumbling cynically to myself, I strutted off in search of another drink. To my mind, it was absurd he should think he had a right to feel offended, or unforgiving.

I don't remember how it came about but at one stage I ended up living with one of my fiancés' brothers, his wife and their baby son. Maybe I thought it was a way of staying close to my elusive shadow. But it didn't last long. While there my scary thoughts spiralled out of control. It was a torture I couldn't keep down, especially at night. There'd been too much degradation, humiliation and violence, and I had no sense of anchorage.

Alone and plagued by thoughts of menacing dark spirits, I swallowed a handful of pills. I wanted the pain to end, but at the same time, I was terrified of dying. There was no guarantee I would be extinct after it was over. I was frightened of what hideous things might be waiting for me on the other side.

I spent the night in the hospital. My parents were informed and collected me the following morning. They took me home and I was visited by the local policeman who tried to offer something along the lines of concerned advice.

It wasn't a serious suicide attempt, but it was a serious cry for help. All I wanted was a normal life, a day to pass without the fear and darkness that lurked behind everything. I did not want to see images of my own violent death anymore; where my blood would be gruesomely splattered up walls and my bloodied face smeared across a window. I was tired of running from my own impending annihilation.

My painful addiction to my ex-fiancé didn't end until I fully experienced the realisation of my mortality in his presence. One night, we came together one last time at the hotel. After closing, he and I started walking to his parents' house. To get there, we had to cross the railway line that ran through the town in the middle of a wide stretch of bushland. He was drunk and angry. Some other man had looked at me and I knew I was going to get hit.

But something seemed different. Instinctively I kept out of arms reach because I could sense a frenzied change in him. He was screaming and calling me filthy names. I began to yell back, standing up for myself and telling him I'd done nothing wrong. The feeling of threat intensified as he tried to come closer, but I kept backing away, feeling violent rage radiate from him.

Suddenly he lunged at me. I screamed, and at the same time a car horn sounded loudly close by, startling both of us. My father pulled up alongside the edge of the road near to where we stood in the scrub. It had been a still summers' night and he'd heard our voices carry clear across town on his way home from the club after locking up. I couldn't run fast enough to get into the car, overwhelmed with gratitude for his miraculous appearance. I knew I'd escaped something I wouldn't have survived had he not shown up when he did. That night my father saved my life. He was my guardian angel.

Everything ended. As popular as my parents were with the Club clientele they'd had enough of drama, gossip and aggravation. They decided it was time to move on after my father was offered a job to run a hotel back in the city.

I decided not to go with them. My ex-fiancé had left town and had been gone for some time. I was finally free of him and free of my family. I'd been re-employed at the local hotel after yet another change of ownership, and was living in the staff quarters. I loved my room. My small space was home. It was light, sunny and safe. My life was behind the bar and I'd made friends with two new staff members who also had rooms in the staff quarters.

My parents gone, I was alone for the first time in my life. It was a strange feeling, infused with a fresh sense of newness and release.

One afternoon between shifts at work, I unexpectedly ran into my ex-fiancés' mother in the main street of town. Seeing her threw me off guard. I was even more rattled by the words of attack that came flying out of her mouth. In retaliation and angry self-defence, I said something nasty about her son, at which point she launched herself at me. Terrified, I turned and ran back to the safety of the hotel. As short as she was she was more than capable of giving me a good hiding.

Once through the hotel's front door I headed straight for the office. Thankfully the door was open. I flew in and locked it behind me. Seconds later my assailant was hurling abuse at me from the other side of the door, letting me know she intended to send for relatives from the neighbouring district. I knew if I was going to remain in one piece I had to leave as soon as possible.

I rang the police and reported what had happened. Crying and frightened I rang my father. I didn't know what else to do or how I was going to get out. He told me to pack my things and stay put. He would come and get me.

My best friend and a male buddy who'd been close with my younger brother, waited with me. They both decided to come along for the ride and to stay with us for a few days.

By the time my father arrived it was dusk. I was relieved to see him and eager to go, but dad had no intention of leaving right away. He'd been drinking and was in the mood to sit at the bar with people he knew and drink some more. My friends and I waited, and waited, until it became clear we had to take control.

Once we got him out the pub door it was obvious he was in no state to drive. We decided my brother's friend should drive instead. As a farm boy he'd learnt to drive at an early age. Even though he didn't have a license, he was by far the safest option.

However, my father was adamant about driving and wouldn't relinquish control of the car. We physically wrestled with him to try to take the keys out of his hands, but he was much too strong and aggressive. Giving in, we set off, me in the front next to my father and my friends in the back.

It was a petrifying ride on the dark country roads and my father took a mean delight in frightening us. We tried to talk, keep things light and friendly, but my father had passed over into one of his sinister moods. It was this side of him that frightened me the most.

We swerved our way towards the city, stopping once to get petrol, something to eat and go to the toilet. With dad out of the car we again tried to get the keys. His driving and his mood had become even more erratic. We failed.

I was so scared I could only breathe in short, controlled gasps. I kept my eyes on the road trying to anticipate the weaving of the car. We rounded a blind corner in the middle of the road and suddenly lights appeared dead ahead as a huge freight truck loomed. I screamed and yelled at dad to get the car back on the right side of the road, but he laughed at my fear.

The oncoming lights glared blindingly through our windscreen. I looked across at my father and saw his threatening pleasure in having the power at his fingertips to decide whether we lived or died. I pleaded, "Dad?"

In a hushed and menacing tone, he responded "Don't worry, you're not going to die tonight." Suddenly, he jerked the steering wheel to the left, pulling us out of the truck's path with only seconds to spare.

By the time we reached the city and made our way to the hotel where my parents lived and worked, I was numb and disassociated. I greeted my mother and put in my order for take-away dinner along with the rest of the family.

Bruised and battered in ways I had no comprehension of, I spent the next four years wandering the countryside as a live-in barmaid, unable to settle and never staying longer than a few months in any one place. By the time I came to know the people and my environment, the uncomfortable, inexpressible crawling that lived in my body would work its way to the surface. While occupied with the novelty of a new situation, I was temporarily distracted from it.

Between jobs I'd come home for a while and sometimes work behind the bar for my father, revelling in the attention of being his daughter, but I never stayed long. Whenever I saw my little sister I felt confused and concerned.

My twenty-first birthday came in a state of depression. I felt old and regretted having done nothing with my life. Other people my age were making plans, had normal lives, boyfriends, love and unity with other people, while I was a rolling stone that didn't fit anywhere.

My birthday was no more special than any other day. I was working away, had a party with the people I associated with in the town, got very drunk drinking a concoction called Rusty Nails, and had another party with my family on my next weekend off. The people there were my parents' friends, my sisters and my brothers with their respective girlfriends, and a couple of stragglers from the bar.

While I was away on one of my live-in country jobs, my parents won the million-dollar lottery in a syndicate of ten. With their share of the winnings they bought a house in the suburbs. It was the first time they had owned a home of their own. When my father rang and told me the news I cried, believing it was heaven-sent compensation for the hardship he and my mother endured, when he went to prison for something he didn't do.

I missed having a family and was always happy to go home between jobs, especially once they moved into the house, but when I did my fantasy of home was always shattered by the truth. My father was still an alcoholic, my mother still raged in the mornings, and lovelessness still lived etched into everyone's faces.

My younger brother followed in my elder brother's footsteps. He joined the Navy and went interstate. My middle sister married the first boy to come along and celebrated her nineteenth birthday on her honeymoon. She'd never had a job or a life of her own outside the malady of our family. It was her escape, running away to the country to be a farmer's wife. It left my youngest sister home alone with my parents.

It took years to get over being my little sister's mother, then not being her mother. I always had the feeling that as a sister/mother, I'd let her down. As adults we've had a close relationship, but it's been a relationship filled with pain and bewilderment over who we are for each other.

I continued to hide in one empty town after another with a solitude I thought I might perish from. Hotels became a trail of temporary homes.

My bedrooms were typical old-fashioned country, furnished with a single bed, a dressing table, wardrobe and night table, all made of the same varnished, dark brown wood. There was something comforting about their polished and ordered sterility. It matched my own. I always kept my room and myself neat and meticulously clean.

I had few belongings, only my clothes, a small stack of treasured records and a cheap stereo system I'd proudly paid off on hire purchase.

When I was not working behind the bar, my facade would drop away and, in my room, locked into quiet emptiness, I would feel the pain of being with myself. Sometimes I had one-night stands just to hold off the inevitability of being alone in the dark, but they were never a gratifying experience, not in any sense. They only intensified my feelings of longing, shame and loneliness.

I always had a peculiar sensation of not being alive. Many times, on a quiet afternoon behind the bar, I'd stare out the window and wonder what lay beyond my vision, questioning if it held anything better than the way I lived. I didn't make friends and was not usually welcomed by the female population of the towns I went to. I was an interloper and looked down on because I was a barmaid.

On visits home, I often went shopping with my mother. I'd stare out the passenger side window of her car as we drove along the streets, trying to see through the walls of the houses we passed, silently asking the same question of every house, "Does love live in there?" The need to know what lay behind the walls, if it was any different to what I had experienced, gnawed at me. I wanted to know how other people lived.

For a while I worked in the Northern Territory where I continued to live the pretence of being a real person. Even so, it was a welcome change from wheatbelt country and over the years, I met many people with names and faces I don't remember. Hiding the truth of who I thought I was from myself and those around me, I worked hard at cultivating an existence, until at twenty-three; I met the man I would marry.

Chapter 4

PRINCE CHARMING

AT some stage in their lives, most girls dream of a fairy tale prince, the one man who will sweep them off their feet and treat them like a princess. Together they will make a home and build a life.

I never had that dream. Instead, I was terrified of having to fulfil a man's expectations in a long-term situation. There was something threatening about it. Instinctively I must have known I pretended my way through life, and that I'd only be good for short-term stage performances.

I'd tried to imagine what it would be like to be married. I'd pictured the bedroom and shuddered with dread at the implication of having to perform over and over for the rest of my life. There would be no escape. The whole idea was too frightening.

I wanted to be loved, but I didn't know what being loved felt like. I only knew what it was like to have a man hurt me or use my body for sex. I had no practice in what would be considered, 'normal life', so was not prepared for the way in which my life was about to change.

I'd left the Northern Territory and was working and boarding in the small hotel of a farming district. It was no different to any other place I'd been, and my reason for being there was no different. It was as good a place as any.

After settling in and the initial stimulation of yet another new situation wearing off, I was more restless and emptier than I had ever been before. I was now twenty-three and it seemed the older I got, the harder it got. I was getting tired of the way I lived my life.

I hadn't been in the town long when the local shire contracted the services of a foreman from the city to build a swimming pool adjacent to the local squash courts. He was put up as a guest in the hotel, and after work, he'd come into the bar and mix jovially with the people.

My first impression of him was unfavourable. There was something about him I didn't like, but eventually we began talking. I was a very polished bar person and always chatted brightly to the customers. Both single, we began to spend time together, playing squash during the day and drinking red wine at night.

We talked about all sorts of meaningless things and within a few short weeks, our friendship unintentionally became a relationship. Lying on my bed, flirting and talking one night after I'd finished work, he asked me what I was thinking. Ever the lonely actress, I sheepishly replied that I wondered what it would be like to kiss him.

We spent the night together and I awoke the next morning to his assumption we were now an item. I tried to tell him it was a mistake, I didn't want to be with him that way, but I couldn't get the words all the way out. Each time I tried I felt overwhelmed by the fear of hurting his feelings. He seemed needy and boyish and his emotional reaction of hurt made me feel bad. Somehow, he was more valid than I was.

I pushed my feelings aside and became involved in the idea of having someone who really seemed to like me. He was kind and affectionate and listened to my poetry with attentive interest. As the weeks passed, I began to feel a sense of familiarity.

I let him move into my room. While I worked at night he would be upstairs doing my ironing. When my shift was over he'd be waiting with soft lights and my favourite Pan Flute track ready to play. After a nice hot shower, I'd slip into bed and he'd gently put headphones over my ears and tell me to lay back and relax. It couldn't have turned out more perfect.

I came to like the attention, the affection and the romance. It was in huge contrast to the way my life had been before his arrival. Until then, working behind the bar was the only place I didn't feel lost.

Sundays had been the worst days. I'd work the morning session and the afternoon, but in between it was as if I was the only person alive on the planet. The little country town went distressingly quiet, with families staying in their homes or congregating at the lake a few miles out of town. I would sit in my room or out on the balcony of the hotel and watch the dust get blown around by the dry summer wind. Sometimes I got in my car and drove the bush roads and tracks, looking, hoping to find something. It made the isolation I felt even more piercing.

The thoughtful things being done for me now changed all that. My barrenness disappeared with something tangible to take its place. I was beginning to feel special and sometimes wore one of his shirts, a statement of possession and belonging. But it was like I was playing in a game, not real life at all.

The affection I initially enjoyed soon became smothering. My boyfriend insisted we fall asleep at night with our arms and legs wrapped around each other. I'd wake in the morning to find myself on the very edge of the mattress facing away from him. I felt like I was being swallowed by his need for constant touching and closeness. Sometimes I got so agitated and angry I just wanted to explode, but I couldn't. I stuffed my feelings down instead and made little excuses about why I needed space.

Our relationship began to change. As I started to pull away in an attempt to keep my sense of separateness, the loving doting man slowly became jealous and possessive and a nasty side emerged. Our friendship began to explode with arguments and manipulations of my autonomy. Yet part of me felt grown up to be in a real relationship. I was especially dazzled by the fact that he even let me drive his car.

Not long after my boyfriend had moved into my room, I discovered he'd lied to me about being single. A woman in the city he'd told everyone was his housekeeper, turned out to be his partner and the mother of his two-year-old son. She had found out about me by coming across a poem

I'd written for him, put away among his things on one of his weekend trips back to the city. All hell broke loose.

I knew he had been divorced and had a daughter from his marriage, and knew he had a child from a de-facto relationship, a relationship I'd been told was long over. But the woman was in fact still living in his house, still under the impression they were a couple, and still sleeping in their bed.

The explanation I was given was that she stayed in his home under joint agreement as his housekeeper, so he could still have contact with his son. Christmas was coming up and he wanted to spend it with him. Their plan was that she would move out after Christmas into a place of her own. She did not still share his bed but had moved into the spare room. According to him she was just jealous and trying to cause trouble.

I believed the story because I could not imagine he would lie about something like that. He was a caring man and loved children. He'd taken immense pride in showing me the little medallion hanging from his key ring with the inscription, 'A man never stands as tall as when he stoops to help a child'. He'd shed tears the day he told me about the daughter he'd lost to divorce.

Yet this woman was responding to our getting together like any woman would if she'd just found out her man, the father of her child, was cheating on her. I felt dazed and torn by the sudden turn of events. My quiet, lonely, country existence had become a soap opera, and I was one of the stars.

My boyfriend stuck with his story, stressing this woman was simply trying to break us up because she wanted him back. I received frequent abusive phone calls from her. She'd call me a slut and go into a tirade about what a bastard my boyfriend was, and how bad my parents must be for raising a daughter like me. It didn't make sense. If she loved him so much and wanted to be with him, why was she telling me so vehemently what a rotten person he was? Her behaviour seemed to add validity to the story that she really was simply jealous and vengeful because he wouldn't take her back.

Christmas arrived. I went home to spend it with my family. My boyfriend went back to his place to be with his son, ex-defacto, and another couple they'd previously arranged to have over for Christmas dinner. But on Christmas Eve night, he phoned to say there'd been a terrible fight. An hour later he pulled up skew whiff on my parent's front lawn, drunk but happy to be with me. My family made him welcome and he fitted right in, no questions asked.

Christmas day was fun and for the first time I had a partner to be my other half among the family. My boyfriend took an instant liking to my big burly brothers. The men drank and played pool, the women cooked, talked, and laughed at the antics of the men. It was a great day.

The festivities over, my boyfriend and I went back to our jobs in the country town. We moved out of the hotel and into a rented house. Our living together was now a more formal and public arrangement. I began to play house. I bought pot plants, cooked and cleaned, and got a little grey kitten I named Smokey to complete the pretty picture. But even Smokey became a bone of contention as my boyfriend's continuing jealousy extended to me having a pet. I was blasted if I fed it in the mornings before making his cup of tea, and for loving and patting it too much or too often.

My boyfriend's changed behaviour baffled me. I thought it was my fault, and if I could just figure out what went wrong and how to fix it, we could get back to the way it had been in the beginning. But as the days and weeks passed, the fighting only accelerated. I was constantly being criticised, interrogated and accused of going behind his back with a local guy I'd dated a couple of times before we'd met. It made me feel crazy. In front of other people he was always so nice, but the minute we were on our own, he would become attacking, hurtful and nasty.

As distressed as I was about the eruption of hostilities and arguments, I couldn't leave. I was well and truly overcome and entangled in being responsible for the circumstances of my boyfriend's life and his feelings. He'd told me all about his ex-wife and the suffering he'd gone through losing his family, how she'd hurt him financially, and the history he'd had with the ex-defacto. They had always had an unstable relationship and for that reason he'd told her he would never marry her. According to him, she'd tried to trap him into marriage by getting pregnant with their son.

My birthday came around. I was about to turn twenty-four and to celebrate; my boyfriend took me away for an overnight stay at a beach resort. After a lovely romantic dinner, we returned to our hotel room and while wrapped happily around each other, he asked me to marry him. Without batting an eyelid, I excitedly said yes. I was so lucky to have someone ask.

The following week I was wearing an engagement ring that signified to me the beginnings of a normal life, the kind other people had. Once we were married, everything would settle down. The ex-defacto would be out of the picture and he would be nice again.

Of course, the illusion of better days didn't last. I found myself increasingly torn over the way I was being controlled and manipulated. The conflict and his jealousy worsened and as it did, I experienced shuddering moments of unnerving similarities to my last relationship, though without the physical violence, I couldn't quite pinpoint what they were. It was just an awful feeling that churned my stomach. I constantly felt anxious and nauseated. What made it worse was the nagging suspicion I'd been lied to about the woman in the city. I spent much of my time in tears, oppressed and ensnared by my own stupidity.

I became emotional, weak and tired as the barrage of sarcasm and belittling remarks wore me down. Feeling ill and suffering sore and painful breasts, I went to the local doctor who put me on a supplement he felt might help with my breast tenderness. When it didn't I went back and was referred for a mammogram in the neighbouring town.

Once there, I was asked if I might be pregnant. That idea had never occurred to me, to my knowledge it was impossible. Sadly, after hearing about the severity of the infection I'd had when I was younger, my gynaecologist had told me it was highly unlikely I'd ever have children.

He'd advised my tubes would have been too badly damaged. Still, this new doctor wanted to be sure, so did a pregnancy test.

After a five-minute wait in reception I was called back into the doctor's office. Feeling rather foolish I waited for him to speak. There was no way I could be pregnant.

"Well, the results positive. Congratulations."

Not knowing what that meant I asked, "What does positive mean?"

"It means you're pregnant and calculated from your last period I'd say you're about six weeks."

Outside the surgery I sat in my car in stunned silence. Pregnant! Disbelieving, I repeated the word out loud, over and over, until unexpectedly I broke out in a smile a Cheshire cat would have been proud of. I'd realised it had been six weeks since my boyfriend and I spent my birthday weekend at the resort. Our child had been conceived the night my fiancé proposed to me. It was so wonderfully romantic.

All the things wrong about my relationship and the situation I was in, disappeared. I was going to have a baby. I'd never been on the pill and had not fallen pregnant before. It just seemed as though this was meant to be, confirmation my fiancé was 'the one', handpicked by God himself. Patting my tummy, I resolved to put everything I had into making my relationship work.

My future husband was excited when he heard the news. The pregnancy brought our marriage plans forward. Invitations were sent out and the details attended to. But my determination to be happy soon crumbled as I began to feel more and more trapped with a man who made me terribly unhappy with his tantrums and dominating behaviour. I was filled with unease and fear.

Panicked, I asked if we could put the wedding off for a while, trying to buy enough time to figure out how I was going to save myself from the impending deadlock of marriage, but the response I received was one of outright anger. He was livid about the way it would make him look to his pommy friends back in the city, and said it was too late anyway, everything had already been organised.

In the face of his tirade and use of guilt to make me feel unreasonable and selfish, I settled to my fate, dropping any thought of not going through with the wedding. I prayed somehow it would all work out.

I couldn't turn to my family for support. I knew the sort of response I'd get if I did, especially from my mother. There would be no words of caring, concerned advice. The pain of being forced to have an abortion at sixteen resurfaced. I was not about to have another one. When I did tell her all she said was, "Well, he'd better marry you because you can't come here."

It suddenly dawned on me that now I was an adult. This time my mother could not control my body. It felt good to have a sense of being apart from her and out of her jurisdiction. For the first time I felt a degree of separateness from the power of my family. They could not do anything to me anymore. I was coming into a life of my own. I had a man who wanted to marry me, and I was going to have a child.

Morning sickness struck, and I was too ill to keep working at the hotel. The slightest whiff of cigarette smoke or stale beer had me dry-retching. I couldn't eat, couldn't drink tea or coffee, or stand the smell of my fiancé's shoes or his sickly-sweet aftershave.

Pangs of fear surfaced about not being able to control the changes to my body, and my need to make myself vomit after I'd eaten became more frequent. It was something I'd been doing secretly for some time as a way of trying to manage my weight.

Everything was changing and seemed so fragile. I stopped playing squash and stopped doing my aerobics routine for fear of losing my baby. I was home alone all day feeling lost not being at work. It was all I knew. My fiancé joined the darts club at the hotel. He'd come home from practice nights reeking of the rancid smells of the bar. I would feel violently ill and beg him to shower off before coming to bed, but he'd refuse, telling me I was being ridiculous.

His unwillingness to care about my needs made me feel ugly and unacceptable. I had the idea that when a man loves a woman he cherishes her, and when carrying his child, it would be a special time of bonding and togetherness. But as the morning sickness worsened, I began to belch constantly with terrible indigestion. Instead of understanding and acceptance, I received disdain and was continually called a pig. When I cried from the hurt of his cruel remarks, I was told I was being pathetic.

I sold my car and put the money towards the wedding. My last source of independence gone, I was now well and truly stuck, miles away from everything and becoming more conquered as the days passed. It seemed the only way I could get along with my boyfriend without conflict, was if I behaved in a way that was compliant, but I couldn't do it. I continued to argue for what I needed and thought we'd had before all the trouble started. The arguments always went around in circles, without anything ever being resolved.

My need to vomit intensified as the changing shape of my body brought on greater bouts of anxiety and panic. I couldn't cope with the way my tummy was expanding and not being able to do up buttons and zips on my jeans so easily. Everything was getting tight. I was fat and ugly and nothing I wore could hide it. Having two things in my belly, food and a growing foetus, made me feel revoltingly full and heavy. Unwilling to get rid of the baby, I got rid of the food.

One afternoon, I was so lonely and in need of reassurance, I went to visit my boyfriend at the site where the swimming pool was being built. As I entered the office, the daughter of the couple who owned the roadhouse café made a sudden exit, and I felt distinctly uncomfortable, as though I'd walked in on something I wasn't supposed to see. When challenged about it, my fiancé defensively denied she was anything but a friend. Anxious about what it might mean if I pushed it, I let the matter go. Better to accept the lie than blow apart my precarious existence with the truth.

Chapter 5

THE SAVIOUR OF MARRIAGE

WITHIN six months of meeting, my boyfriend and I had married, left the wheatbelt, and moved into a unit in the city. I was three months pregnant on the day of our wedding and finally over trying to control my body. The changes were inevitable. The day after our wedding, I relaxed my tummy for the first time, relieved to feel as though I didn't have to hold it in any longer. I was legitimate.

I knew my marriage was a mistake, but it was a clouded knowing, obscured by all the fear I'd accumulated over the course of my life. I was oblivious to any real feelings or desires, other than a concealed self-revulsion. I had no dreams or ambitions. I was a blob, moulded and shaped by the winds and storms of other people's lives, driven by an unconscious need to constantly keep moving.

On the day of my wedding, I gained more than a husband. I gained an image of normalcy and respectability. I had everything I thought I was never going to have, a home, a family and a future. From the time of my twenty-first birthday I'd had many moments of dread where I'd tried to visualize myself in the future, only to be staring into an immeasurable, black and barren void. I had thought it meant I was going to die young.

Like a chameleon, I blended myself to fit acceptably with my changing circumstances. It was a honed survival skill, something I did without thinking. But when finally forced to stand still and live in one place, be the same person every day, I was no longer able to outrun the churning I'd kept at bay for so long. Slowly it began to break through as I found myself in a role I did not know how to play. My husband and I didn't know each other. We had little in common other than we were both wounded, empty people. Our romance had begun as thoughtless escapism.

Everything I did was wrong. I was constantly chastised, even for locking our front door while home alone. It irritated my new husband to have to go to the trouble of finding and using his keys to unlock it when he got home from work. We argued constantly over stupid and trivial things.

Shortly after the wedding, we received a letter from the celebrant who'd performed our marriage ceremony. It was to inform us she'd neglected to have us sign an important document which should have been signed on the day. It was in the envelope with the letter. She requested we sign it and send it back as soon as possible. Until it was done, our marriage was not legal and binding.

My heart soared at the prospect of being free. My first instinct was to run and never look back, but the bulge in my belly reminded me that I was still pregnant, and with nowhere to go. The realisation stole my exhilaration just as quickly as it had come. I glimpsed the sun, then it was gone.

The document sat on our kitchen bench top for over a week. I didn't want to sign it. I talked to my mother, telling her how unhappy I was and hoping to hear words of guidance and support, but she said I didn't have a choice. I should sign it and make the most of my life. I'd made my bed and now I had to lie in it. I signed my name on the dotted line, but it was done with a feeling of hopeless resignation.

The reality was I didn't know how to deal with the situation I was in. I felt trapped and powerless. Choice was not a concept that existed for me. My life had continually taught me I had no choice. I existed through unconscious knee-jerk reactions and responses to the circumstances of my life, not any level of aware forethought.

I didn't have any measure of personal authority or self-knowledge. I had no capacity to weigh up pros and cons with a clear hold on reality. I couldn't question myself about how right or wrong something or someone might be for me. I didn't know how to make a free choice about anything. I made choices from fear and lack of self.

My husband's ex-defacto and two-year-old son moved out of his house and into a unit in another suburb, and we moved into the house. I hated it. It didn't feel like a home. It felt heavy and sombre. I could sense the debris of his relationships with his first wife and child and his ex-defacto and their child. I felt I had no right to be there. To make matters worse, my new husband let me know in no uncertain terms I was in his territory.

I tried to settle into my new life as a housewife in suburbia with a baby on the way. Being pregnant was the one thing that made everything seem worthwhile, the only thing that made any sense. I mused over how I hoped things would be once our child was born, and focused on the excitement of preparing a nursery. I bought the necessities I needed in the way of maternity clothes, and one or two items of baby clothing each week. I still couldn't believe I was actually a married woman. Having the label made me feel more of a credible person.

But as my pregnancy progressed, a startling realisation I could give birth to a boy began to deeply trouble me. It had to be a girl. It just had to be. Sometimes I had nightmares that raised something dirty from deep in my subconscious, but I couldn't look at what the dreams were about. I just wrestled with my secret terror when it came, and forced it as far away from me as possible.

I often stood in the doorway of the nursery with my hands resting on my growing belly, just looking at the empty bassinet and its pretty lemon-coloured trimmings. It was a practice that drew sarcastic remarks from my husband. He was already showing signs of jealousy toward our unborn child, especially when I fussed and crooned over feeling it kick.

One afternoon, I was lying down on our bed having a rest, when my husband came into the room to change to go out into the garden. I was feeling warm and loving and could feel the baby moving inside me. I reached out my hand and asked if he'd lay with me for a cuddle before going outside, but he turned on me nastily and said he had better things to do than make love to me all day. It seemed I was the only one who thought the life I was carrying was an event to be treasured. Stealing precious moments of loving, non-sexual intimacy was out of the question.

What hurt the most was the day my husband looked at my belly with derision after I'd said I wanted to buy a Christmas present for our baby. It was the month of December and I was due on the nineteenth. It would be our child's first Christmas. He sneeringly responded with, "You're not going to buy that thing a present are you?"

I wanted so much to experience the happiness of being cared for, of being considered and appreciated, like being asked if I would like a coffee periodically, rather than always being told to put the kettle on to make him one. Or being allowed to sleep in every now and then and be surprised by breakfast in bed, rather than the unspoken expectation I always got up first to wait on him. Be given a cuddle for no other reason than to say, I like who you are and am glad you're here, as opposed to, I want sex. My husband always pushed me away during the day when I put my arms around him for a hug. I wanted to connect, but he reserved our connecting for the bedroom. I felt hurt most of the time. What I wanted on the inside, I couldn't manifest on the outside.

The more I got to know my husband, the more I grew to dislike who he was. I didn't like the way he was so judgmental and verbally abusive about other drivers on the road. He picked at everything, the speed they drove, the way they changed lanes, even a person's ethnicity, and he particularly disparaged women drivers. Sometimes he'd speed up and block people off, tailgate, or verbally rant out loud about someone who had the audacity to break a road rule to get in front of him, and when I was the one behind the wheel and he the passenger, he criticised everything I did until I was a nervous wreck and couldn't think for myself.

He was at his worst after drinking on the odd night out. I would have to drive home with him in my ear. "You're driving too fast, you're driving too slow, get in the left lane, don't take corners like that you'll damage the tyres, don't change gears like that you'll wear the gearbox, don't use the brakes like that it chews through fuel." And if I was driving in an area I didn't know and he was giving directions, he'd give them to me right at the last moment, and rant if I got it wrong or took a corner too sharp.

Sometimes I had to give directions from the road map while he drove, but I'd get confused and flustered and he'd yell and tell me how stupid I was. I'd never used one before and didn't know how to read it fast enough for his liking. My brain would blitz out, he'd wrench the road map from me, pull over to the side of the road and disgustedly get the directions himself.

Shopping was a chore I did on my own and always on a Saturday morning when I could use the car. It was a menial task and strictly 'women's business.' I'd come home with loads of groceries and fresh pastries from the bakery for lunch. Saturday was a treat day, though the most important things were my husband's newspaper and lotto tickets.

But there were occasions when I'd forget to go to the newsagent. Sometimes I found it hard to focus. I'd have peculiar feelings of agitation. When I forgot, my husband would explode into a tirade of belittling criticism for my being so stupid, then start on how poorly I stacked the groceries in the cupboard. He'd proceed to take them all out and stack them back - his way. All labels had to face the front and all items had to be stacked according to size, large things at the back with a progressive sizing that graduated down to the smallest items.

Everything had to be neat and orderly and the shelves in the pantry had to be full. If I didn't keep lots of canned and packaged foods, my husband felt I wasn't taking care of him or our household properly. It made him feel poor. He was particular about food and bragged how he'd taught his ex-defacto to never dish up mince. He'd thrown a meal she'd cooked with it in the bin and reprimanded her for dishing up dog food. The fact I got away with it made me feel strangely special, as though I had one up on her.

But I couldn't find a place for myself or my own way of doing things. Everything had to be done the way my husband liked it otherwise I was punished by his withdrawal and silence, sometimes for days at a time.

One More Breath

We never did things together or talked much to each other about anything beyond the surface of day-to-day living. There was so much unsaid. Each week-day morning my husband got out of bed with just enough time to eat, shower, dress and leave for work without speaking a word. I always had to break the silence first. There were never any loving, good-morning greetings.

During the early part of our marriage, I often tearfully and angrily threatened to leave. It was the only way I knew how to get my husband to be nicer to me. He'd look all worried, soften, then talk me round and I would agree to stay, getting his attention back and breaking the stalemates we often found ourselves in. My attempts at manipulation were hollow, but my husband didn't know that. Over time, my empty threats lost their power.

My little kitten Smokey had grown into a beautiful cat. I loved her, but my husband had only ever tolerated her. One sunny Saturday afternoon we went to get in the car to go out. I noticed Smokey lying behind it in the middle of the driveway, snoozing in the warmth of the day, and pointed her out, asking my husband to move her. Irritably he refused and told me off for fussing. She'd get out of the way herself when the engine started. Heavily pregnant and already under pressure from my husband's prickly temper, I didn't want to upset him further, so let it go. I hoped he was right, Smokey would move of her own accord.

The car engine started and before I knew it we were flying down the driveway. I felt the bump as we drove over her. Smokey frantically scaled the side fence and shot into our back yard. When I screamed my husband stopped the car, but my display of distress infuriated him. I got out and ran in search of her, finding her crouched underneath a Geraldton Wax bush in our back yard.

Outwardly Smokey seemed alright, but she was cringing and wide-eyed, and her breathing was laboured. I insisted on taking her to a vet not far from where we lived. Once in the waiting room, I started to relax and feel better. There were no open wounds or bleeding. Then suddenly, a large amount of brownish fluid mixed with blood gushed from her bowel. The vet did all he could, but Smokey died during surgery.

In the early hours of December 3rd, 1984, my waters broke. My husband was annoyed at being woken, but I was excited. I pushed my hurt at his lack of enthusiasm aside and concentrated on getting my breathing right. I needed to deal with the pain. My contractions were already five minutes apart. There was no time to indulge in feeling upset. Two and a half hours later, a brand-new human being was being pulled from my body, and as the baby came into full view, I was overwhelmed with relief to see it was a girl.

I was in awe on my tiny daughter. She was exquisite, a soft pink rosebud, just waiting to flower. I had carried her inside my body. Now here she was in my life, in my arms, no longer an idea but a reality. Having the experience of feeling her grow, embracing the changes to my body after my earlier unease, and ultimately giving birth, felt like an amazing achievement.

But my joy felt empty without a loving partner to share it with. The moment I'd been transferred from the birthing suite to the ward on the upper floor, my husband left, saying he had to go to work. I never saw him again until late that evening, and then only briefly. No flowers, no special mark of the occasion of our child's entrance into the world.

For the first twenty-four hours I couldn't sleep, unable to take my eyes off the miracle in the cot beside me. It was astonishing to me that she was mine. In the drawer next to my bed I found a Bible. Thumbing through its pages, I spoke a heartfelt prayer of thanks with an immense sense of gratitude, even though deep inside I believed myself to be utterly unworthy.

I was eager to take our daughter home and begin our lives as a family. I left the hospital four days after the birth. The picture I had in my mind of how I hoped it would be was idyllic. My husband would soften; melt at the sight of our baby girl and become more loving. We would exchange devoted glances and share our pleasure of her together, delighting in the wonderful life we'd created.

But the unrealistic fantasy I'd allowed myself to believe in was an illusion. My husband was barely interested in our daughter. His attention toward her did not extend beyond the superficial coo and tickle. Nothing and no one took precedence over himself or his work, be it his job or house and gardens.

I found myself alone all day with a baby who screamed in agony for hours on end with severe colic. Most feeds became projectiles as she vomited everything up. She hardly ever slept, which meant I never slept. Sleep deprived and stressed, I felt overwhelmed and received little tolerance or support from my husband. Anytime I looked to him for relief or help, I was angrily rebuffed.

We did nothing but fight. My husband was cranky and put out that we had to wait six weeks before having sex. I needed time for my stitches to heal. I'd torn badly due to the fast and unprepared way my daughter chose to make her entrance into the world.

I came to hate my husband touching me. Mostly he was impatient, unkind and unloving, making it impossible for me to feel safe, happy or sexual towards him. But I acted in the way expected. If I didn't he would withdraw for days at a time and sulk like a child. Mostly I felt nothing from him except disapproval, towards me and our little girl.

I had expected so much from married life. I'd brought nothing into it except unrealistic fantasies and expectations which were progressively being shattered. I lacked knowledge, experience and understanding. I'd made assumptions about how things would be and should be.

Our first outing with our baby, carefully swaddled and proudly tucked in her carry bassinet, was to a Chinese restaurant for an early dinner. As my husband and I sat across from one another, the distant silence between us had me fighting back tears. We had nothing to say. It made my throat constrict and my heart ache. I was sad I didn't have a close, loving relationship with the father of my child.

To compound my unhappiness, I began having strange thoughts in the early weeks following my daughter's birth. I found myself increasingly anxious and self-conscious whenever I changed her nappy after she'd soiled. Having to touch her so intimately made me feel uncomfortable, as if I was doing something wrong. What if my hand lingered too long?

Shocked and repulsed, I wondered if I was crazy. My deeply held secret that I was a vile creature began to re-emerge, along with old fragmented memories that haunted me as I tried to be a good mother. I feared if anyone knew what I was thinking, what I was terrified of becoming; my daughter might be taken from me. I struggled with feelings of being too sullied to have a child.

I knew I would never do anything to hurt my baby, or ever want to, yet my unspoken past and intrusive what if thoughts suggested otherwise. It could be in my blood, lurking like a virus.

I was deeply disturbed by what was going through my mind. I had no one to confide in, no one to help me understand what was happening. I desperately wanted to talk to someone, but my shame was already more than I could stand. I had to keep it to myself and lock the badness out. I had to stay one-step ahead of it.

As my baby grew, I was unable to be the soft, loving mother I wanted to be. Short-tempered and barely coping, I couldn't provide a loving family home. I didn't know how. Drowning on my own, I was in angry turmoil and fell miles short of the expectations I had for myself.

For the most part I felt like I didn't know what I was doing. I blundered through each day, feeling panic stricken and inadequate. When my baby wasn't crying I didn't know what to do with her, how to relate to or play with her.

Sometimes we had visitors and the moment the house began to bustle with other people, my daughter would become scared and cry uncontrollably. The only way to calm her down would be to take her out of the room. She seemed to be particularly frightened of my father. He was not able to come anywhere near her.

Struggling financially as well as emotionally, letters from the Child Support Agency began to roll in, threatening to take furniture from our home for falling behind in the maintenance payments my husband had to pay for his other two children. My father was diagnosed with throat cancer and my breast milk dried up from stress, putting an end to three months of fumbled, anxiety-ridden breast-feeding.

Around the time our daughter was fourteen months old, I was surprised to discover I'd fallen pregnant again. The knowledge set me to dreaming and I romanticised the idea of having another baby. But bulimia had well and truly re-surfaced and the strain of forced vomiting caused me to miscarry at six weeks. The fantasy had been short-lived and though I felt sad, I acknowledged it was probably for the best.

Unsettled and restless, I needed something in my life to ease the stifled and insulated way I felt. I wanted to go back to work and used our money troubles as leverage. My husband couldn't argue. I rang our local Tavern and was lucky enough to get a casual bar job.

Back in familiar territory, I felt a longing for the anonymous simplicity of my old life. Suddenly it was preferable to the unhappy situation I was in now. My husband hated me working and sometimes told me I looked like a slut when I dressed nice and wore makeup for work. I felt miserable. I couldn't be happy and he couldn't be happy with me.

I only worked weekend nights so my husband could look after our daughter. He detested it. To him it was inconvenient babysitting rather than team-work or parenting. I would have the meals organised and everything ready so it would be easy for him, but he never made it easy for me. He was unkind and gruff to our daughter, making me feel torn about leaving her. I knew it was retribution, but I couldn't bring myself to believe he continued his antics after I left.

When I got home I always asked in a happy, friendly voice how things had been while I was gone and if our daughter had been good for him. The answer was always the same. She was a little bitch, wouldn't eat her dinner, and cried all the time. I hated my life and began to despise my husband for the unloving and intolerant way he was as a father.

I fell pregnant again. A blood test confirmed the pregnancy and I attended my first ultrasound. But there was no baby to be seen. My doctor said I must have miscarried, and as I hadn't bled, the tissue must have been reabsorbed back into my body. To make sure nothing remained to cause infection, I underwent a day stay in hospital to have my uterus scraped. However, as the days went by I could have sworn I was still pregnant.

Two weeks passed before something exploded in my left side, dropping me to the floor with intense, indescribable pain. Frightened, I rang my sister-in-law, who rushed me to our local hospital.

The hospital's attending gynaecologist was called to see me. After some poking, prodding, and responsive gasps of sharp pain from me, it was pronounced I needed to be admitted right away.

Immediately I felt rocked by feelings of panic. I knew this would upset and irritate my husband. But what stunned me most was the sudden, rising dread I felt about our daughter being left alone with him.

I lay in the hospital bed all day, getting weaker and weaker as the hours passed. My sister-in-law had long gone, taking my daughter with her. My own gynaecologist was called in. The two doctors stood out in the corridor arguing over my prognosis. The hospital's doctor was concerned I'd suffered a tubal rupture from an undiagnosed ectopic pregnancy. My doctor said it was impossible. He'd scraped my uterus after my miscarriage and had checked my fallopian tubes during the procedure.

In the meantime, I was left alone, and no action was taken. By nine p.m. that night, a strange and frightening stillness had come over me. I couldn't move my body, and when the night nurse came in, I feebly begged her to help me.

I couldn't decide if I was cold or not as I was wheeled down the dim corridor. It seemed like I should be cold, but I couldn't feel much of anything. The room I was taken into shone extraordinarily bright after the dark ride through the corridors. It was sparse, sterile and silver. I was lifted and put onto the operating table.

The next morning I woke up with a belly full of stitches. The nurse who tended me told me I was a very lucky woman. I'd lost a lot of blood. The hospital's gynaecologist came in to see me and explained he'd been right. I'd had an ectopic pregnancy that ruptured the fallopian tube at eight weeks gestation. Internal scarring of the tube was noted as the cause, and I was told any following pregnancy put me at substantial risk of another ectopic event.

My body healed and I went back to work. Arguments became more frequent and intense as my husband's attitude toward our daughter became ever more hostile. Eating together at the kitchen table at night often ended with him getting up in disgust and taking his meal to the lounge room, leaving us rejected and alone, or him telling me to get a nosebag for our daughter so she could eat outside with the animals. He couldn't stand the way she ate with her fingers and frequently called her a pig for not using her spoon. The insanity of it was that our daughter was still in a high-chair, and simply being her age. Once, he upended his own dinner plate in temper, smashing the plate and spraying food all over the floor and wall, scaring our baby girl into a fit of terrified tears. The more I stood between him and our daughter, trying to shield and stand up for her, the more hot-tempered and resentful he became toward both of us.

At work, I started to twirl my wedding ring around my finger as if it was a noose around my neck, wishing I could take it off. I fantasised about having an affair, but in my fantasy I wasn't doing anything bad, just getting swept away in my imagination by the most romantic scenes I could imagine. I wanted intimacy and gentle loving. I wanted to be smiled at and have my face stroked, not be ridiculed and criticised.

I performed well in my job and often received compliments. I always looked presentable and other people saw me as attractive. It made me feel happy and good about myself, restoring some small amount of self-confidence. There were some things I could do right. I would tell my husband with a sense of pride, but his response was always, "The only reason they are giving you compliments is because they're trying to get into your pants."

My husband's remarks made me angry. Wasn't I worth more than just sex? Is that all he could see in me? It seemed I would never get away from that image of myself. It was all I was good for and the only way I could be loved. I decided to never tell him anything about work again, but it made me feel sad. I had nothing separate about me to share with him.

One night after my husband and I had made love, I tried to talk to him openly about how I was feeling. He acknowledged he'd been able to tell something was different about me, and as I lay in his arms, pleased at his perceptiveness and willingness to talk about it, I confessed I was unhappy. But I was unsuspecting of what it was he'd been referring to. He'd meant he could tell I'd had sex with another man, simply by the sex we'd just had. According to him, my body hadn't felt the same, as though another man's penis had somehow changed his own fit. Stunned, all I could do was respond with hurt and indignant anger. For my part, I had wanted to take the opportunity to talk about the way I felt making love, when I felt so unloved by his behaviour.

I began to play out my daydream of having an affair. It was too easy to justify getting chummy with one of the customers at the tavern. He was charming, witty and attractive in a very distinguished, English-looking way. We flirted and talked easily, and in our conversations, I alluded to not being happy in my marriage.

It was obvious he liked me. He asked many times if I'd meet with him for coffee, and though I always politely refused, it was done with a playful indication that maybe next time I might say yes.

A day came when I did agree to meet him, but it wasn't for coffee. It was to go for a stroll on the beach. I had no intention of anything happening between us, in fact, I hadn't thought it through at all. I just wanted some relief from the misery of my squashed and unhappy life. However, once on the beach, I realised I'd made a dreadful mistake.

The beach was deserted except for a few seagulls. The wind was blowing sand through the cool air and I felt deadened and unreal. The conversation took a more intimate turn as we sat on the sand nestled among a crop of small dunes. My friend put his arms around me and drew me close for a kiss.

It didn't feel anything like the romanticised embrace of my imaginings. The wind was sharp and the sand stung my skin. I wanted to go home. As I looked around to see if anyone else was on the beach, my friend assured me no one was about. He lay me down and kissed me again.

I didn't like his kiss and I wasn't attracted to him at all. I moved to get up, saying I didn't want to go any further. I was a married woman with a child I should be at home with. Then the coaxing started, the wheedling, until I lay back down in the sand like a limp rag doll. He slid the crutch of my knickers aside, and within a matter of a minute it was over and done with. I was a robotic receptacle, and what this man wanted was ultimately more important than me, my guilt, or my desire to go home. I straightened myself, he did up his fly, and we headed back to the car.

I don't remember getting home. But I remember being propelled by roiling nausea through my front door and into the shower, frantically stripping my clothes off on the way. I tried to scrub away the dirty sensation I felt all the way to the bone, except it wouldn't wash away. Huddled on the shower floor, with the hot water pelting my body, I cried until I couldn't cry anymore. I felt ashamed and disgusted with what I'd done. The only way I could live with it was to make it disappear. The event simply never happened.

Over time, I began to feel a longing for another child, perhaps stirred by the losses I'd had, or maybe it was because I was trying to fulfil some expectation of what I thought it meant to be a family. But terrible period pain and heavy bleeding plagued me. I went to a specialist and discovered I had endometriosis. After a course of hormonal drug treatment, I fell pregnant again. It was another ectopic, and surgically removed before it could do any damage.

Even though I was working and bringing in a little money, we were still in financial trouble. My husband needed to get a better job because the people he worked for took advantage of him, made promises they didn't keep, and paid him poorly while they lived the high life, even though their company was going under. I knew he was capable of more than what he was doing on the tools as a foreman, and had told him so our first Christmas together. My gift to him had been a tan, leather briefcase with his initials engraved on it in gold lettering.

Looking for a new job was confronting for my husband. He had little belief in himself and was holding on to false hopes with the job he had. He'd look through the paper and come up with nothing, until one day a job description stood out. It was everything he knew how to do and was good at, but the job title was intimidating. An established and dynamic building company was looking for a Project Manager.

I reminded my husband of all the knowledge and skill he had. He had nothing to lose by giving it a go. With a little more encouragement and gentle prodding, he applied for the job.

When my husband received a letter of invitation to attend an interview, he fretted. He had nothing in his wardrobe but worn work clothes, T-shirts and shorts, and the odd casual shirt and pair of jeans. The only suit he owned was an outdated brown velvet suit with flared pants he'd worn the day he married his first wife back in England. He desperately needed a bit of re-styling. Together we went through his wardrobe and threw out the old to make way for the new, a smart, grey, tailored suit bought on sale.

My husband got the job and in a very short time made a huge impression on his new bosses, winning himself in-office awards for excellence. They were so impressed, they sent him interstate to manage the re-vamping of a shopping centre in Melbourne. Without him to look after our daughter, I had to quit my job. My husband was given a company car as part of his package, so I was able to have our car. I could go to the shops anytime during the week and visit my mother whenever I wanted. At last I had a sense of freedom and mobility.

One night while my husband was away, I was doing the ironing in front of the television. Flicking through the channels looking for something interesting to watch, I came across an image of a little girl in a blue dress jumping on a trampoline. Her face had been blurred so I couldn't see what she looked like. A man's voice was talking about how she'd been a victim of violation at the hands of her uncle.

As I watched and listened, I held my breath and my body went rigid. It soon became clear the program was on the topic of Childhood Sexual Abuse, a term I'd never heard before.

The narrator went on to say the uncle was a criminal and had been prosecuted for his crime. As the story continued to unfold, pieces of the wall I'd erected to separate myself from my past, toppled to the ground. Maybe there was more to what I'd always assumed to be true about my own childhood. When the documentary finished, it ended with the names of some organisations to contact should anyone need further information or support. I wrote one down for my area.

My heart began to race as I tried to grasp how this program was relevant to me. Was it possible I'd been a victim? I picked up the phone and rang my husband in Melbourne, getting him out of bed.

The conversation was stilted and uncomfortable. My husband didn't really seem interested in the conversation. Embarrassed, I began to cry. As I fumbled over my words, awkwardly sharing what my uncle and brother had done to me as a child, I already knew I wasn't going to get what I needed. I felt stupid for even trying.

My husband's lack of concern prompted me to ask if it made him feel any different about me. The phone line went quiet. In the stretch of silence, I heard the answer and wasn't surprised when he said, "I suppose it all depends on how old you were at the time, how long it went on, and whether you allowed it."

I hung up the phone and berated myself for making such a silly call. It was my own fault. I should have waited until he got home and told him in person. Then it would have been different, I would have got the caring I'd wanted. Doing it impulsively over the phone, I'd robbed myself. Stupid girl!

But I also felt angry. The narrator from the documentary had said the child was an innocent victim. Hadn't I been just a child? If she was innocent, surely so was I.

Picking the phone up again, I dialled the number I'd taken from the program, and spoke with a woman from a twenty-four-hour sexual assault counselling line. She gave me the comfort, support and validation

I needed. By the end of the call, I realised something had been dragged out of the closet that couldn't be shoved back.

As the days and weeks passed, the conversation I'd had with the counsellor wouldn't let me go. I became unhappier and more discontented, acting my way through every day, going through the motions of being a wife and mother. Nothing I did brought me any joy or fulfilment. Everything was tainted and coloured by what I carried buried and hidden deep inside.

I rang another number provided by the phone counsellor and made an appointment with the Sexual Assault Referral Centre. There I attended my first counselling session, my demeanour guarded as I revealed only selective little bits, testing my safety. I feared what the consequences might be for speaking out, worried I could even have my child taken from me. There was always someone to mete out some kind of punishment, and I was the one usually being punished.

Yet it was here I first heard people telling me I had done nothing wrong. In fact, it was I who'd been wronged. The initial contact and following sessions gave me the courage to attend an eight-week program in group therapy.

I heard about the concept of the Inner Child for the first time and discovered I couldn't relate to myself as ever having been a child. During a relaxation exercise, I was shocked by the physical tension in my body. I needed to keep my eye on the door and know the location of every other person in the room. I was afraid and unable to keep my eyes closed. It was my first objective experience in self-awareness.

By the end of the eight weeks, I felt puzzled and was under the impression I was supposed to be fixed now. But unbeknown to me, all I'd done was scrape the scab off a very old and deep-rooted wound. My history was coming into view, presenting itself to be remembered, grieved, and cleansed.

The resistance from my husband and my family as I tried to reach out for help, made me feel even crazier than I already believed I was. I cried and begged to be understood, without being able to explain the true extent of what I was feeling. At the time I had no words, I did not understand it myself. Gagged and unable to utter the dying I felt inside, I lived with a constant resonating scream in my head that went "aaarrhhhhhhh', like someone trying to speak with their tongue cut out.

Chapter 6

A NEW JOURNEY

Life is ever changing, and when change occurs it can be as much about an aside interruption, as for a new opportunity. With the advent of a better job and income, my husband decided it was time to sell up and move on. I was so grateful and imagined all our troubles being left behind within the walls of his house. We moved in with my parents who lived on the premises of their rural general store, bought a block of land in the hills and set about building a new house.

In exchange for living rent free with my parents, my husband renovated both the store and the adjoining living quarters we all shared. He tore down walls, put in new windows, floor coverings, bathroom and kitchen. It was messy, dusty, challenging work, but it created a sense of fellowship as we all worked together, particularly between my parents and my husband. I often worked in the shop, and usually cooked the evening meals.

However, it didn't take long before living with my parents, particularly my father, dredged up haunting feelings of being small and despised. He still zeroed in on me with hurtful comments laced with contemptuous spite. When he drank his eyes held the same look that had terrified me so much as a child.

If there was a conversation about anything and I gave my opinion, or talked with seeming knowledge on any subject, he would laugh scathingly and tell me to keep my mouth shut unless I had something intelligent to say, sometimes even at the dinner table in front of my husband and our three-year-old daughter. Nothing had changed.

There were poorly veiled, snide remarks comparing me to my middle sister. In my father's eyes she was, by virtue of her status as the attractive 'good' daughter, acceptable, while I was her opposite. He made me feel unacceptable and self-conscious, and even though I was not particularly overweight, I took up aerobics in the lounge room, hoping to improve my appearance and shaky self-confidence. But I was made fun of for supposedly making the walls of the shop shake. Sometimes in the middle of a workout, he'd come through the lounge to use the bathroom, slowing his stride long enough to look my way with a snigger that spoke volumes.

For the most part I liked being around my mother, even though as time went on, an underlying tension began to build between us. It came from all the unspoken things, the old hurts and stories that were buried and hidden. More than at any other time, I talked awkwardly to her about my unhappy marriage, my confusion over what love was and the way my father treated me. I longed for her to be my safe and supportive refuge, a place where I could receive the kind of wisdom and strength only a loving mother could provide.

I began to open up to her about some of things I remembered as a small girl, like the time my father was carried through our front door so drunk he couldn't stand on his own, let alone walk. She'd turned on him, leaving him slumped in a blubbering, dribbling heap on the kitchen floor. Feeling sorry for him, I attempted to comfort him, but as soon as I was within reach, he pulled me down to the ground and kissed me full on the lips, swirling his tongue all around the inside of my mouth. The smell and taste of his saliva filled my nostrils to the point of his rancid breath almost taking over my own. Choking, I had to fight to get away.

The more I talked to my mother the more she began to put a wall between us, distancing herself from any sense of guilt or responsibility. She didn't want to know. Instead, she began to encourage me to take my grievances direct to my father, but that was a frighteningly unthinkable prospect. I didn't want to talk to him; it was her I needed.

Sometimes my daughter went with her grandfather in his white ute to pick up stock feed for the grain shed. I'd watch them leave the driveway with sick feelings and a squirming stomach, not understanding why. Looking for reassurance I tried to bring the subject up with my mother, but she couldn't deal with the conversation.

I told myself I was being absurd. He wasn't a monster. He was my father. He'd never do anything to hurt my beautiful, innocent little girl. How could I even have such thoughts? But as much as I tried to let it go, I could never feel comfortable.

After many long months our home was finally finished, and we moved in. It was good to have a new place of our own, free and uninhabited by the ghosts of anyone's history. My husband surprised me with a ten-thousand-dollar savings book account I didn't know he had, and gave me the task of choosing curtains and new furniture for our house. It was the first time I'd been allowed to have a say that wasn't controlled, manipulated, or directed by him.

However, you cannot bury the past. You cannot move to a new location, a new anything and think for one minute that what you left behind, didn't come with you. What is yours will follow you until you have the courage to look it square in the face. No matter how busy you make yourself or try to cover the truth, it will niggle and annoy until you are either unable or unwilling, to suffer any longer.

Once the dust had settled and the spending was done, our lives slotted into a new order, but it was only the external that had altered. My husband was still moody and critical. When he wasn't at work he was outside in the garden, living in his own world, away from being close to me or our daughter. Three people lived in our house, but there were no real connections other than by physical proximity.

Our daughter couldn't make any noise that was disturbing, especially when the news was on, and innocent, make-believe games with her toys were never tolerated. She got the fright of her life once when sitting on the toilet. For some reason she'd decided to sit back-to-front, facing the cistern rather than the door. She was singing nursery rhymes, innocently lost in her reverie, when suddenly her father burst through the door in a rage, demanding she shut up. She was so frightened she almost fell off the seat.

What had been interrupted by change slowly began to filter back to me, all the old feelings of restless agitation, magnified now by the time spent living with my parents. The arguments, tears, and unrequited longings of my heart for something other, persisted and intensified. My daughter went to pre-school, then primary school, and I blundered on, wandering around my life, bumping into things, always fighting for something. Nothing came easy.

Trying to recall the sequence of events from this point, so I can neatly place them in their right order, is at times, beyond what I can manage. It's such a tangled mess of trauma and blind alleyways, I find it difficult to be in the place of remembrance long enough to pull all the pieces apart from each other. I have an expectation that as an adult, I should be able to remember, but all the pieces are seared unrecognisably together.

Yet I remember well the terrifying feeling of being missing that I lived with. It clutched at me as I tried to be what I was supposed to be, a mother, a wife, a homemaker. I was in one physical location, feeling at the same time as though I were somewhere else. Where was I? Where was it I wanted to be, and why couldn't I feel anything other than anxiety? Why was I out of my depth in caring for my child? Why did I constantly feel like I did not have a clue about what I was doing, and why was I scared to death of authority figures, even my child's teachers?

Looking back, it all makes sense, but at the time nothing was clear. All I knew was that I was unhappy and trapped in a marriage that had never been fulfilling. I couldn't distinguish if I felt that way because I was in the wrong life, with the wrong man, or if my sense of displacement was coming from within me, projecting out.

Eventually, through an acquaintance of my husband, I came to hear about a place called Holyoake. Because of my background, it was suggested I have a look at what the organisation had to offer. It was to be a major turning point. There, I participated in a twelve-step Adult

Child of an Alcoholic program, and began my education in the process of addiction and its impact on the family. More importantly, how it had impacted on me.

I'd grown up believing I was bad, guilty and sinful, with something inherently wrong with me. Through the program I was given another perspective, one that told me I was none of these things, but that my parents and our family as a system, had been sick.

The revelation was like having a blindfold ripped from my eyes without having time to adjust to the explosion of light. On my first night I ran in shocked disbelief from the building, choking on tears, desperately trying to cope with the unexpected welling up of raw emotion. It was more than I could bear. I'd spent my whole life seeing myself as being at fault. It hurt so much, and even more to realise I'd been allowed to think the worst of myself in order for my parents to feel comfortable with themselves.

At Holyoake I discovered the truth about my childhood and my family, the alcoholism, the violence, and the abuse in all its forms. I heard words, stories, phrases and terms that described my life.

In the beginning I would sit in stunned and angry silence during the group sessions. In this place I was not unique, and I saw the other people as rivals for attention. I had to learn to become part of a group. But it wasn't long before Holyoake became a haven that gave me permission to explore the truth, allowing me to relinquish my stories and resentment. I discovered more about my life and myself.

I struggled to adjust my self-concept and integrate a change in my reality. Everything had been turned upside down. More counselling followed as I began to question openly why I was so miserable and unfulfilled in my marriage. I'd always put it down to not liking the way my husband treated me and our child. Now it was being attributed directly to my childhood.

Everything became about my childhood. Any legitimate reasons for my unhappiness in current time disappeared. My husband began to hide behind my history as a way of deflecting the truth about himself and not accept his own faults. My childhood became his weapon against me.

My exposed history replaced my previous view of myself with something much more broken, though now at least I was establishing some context in which I could have a basic understanding of myself. I was beginning to have words that expressed some of the feelings I carried inside, but nowhere near enough to replace the sound of "aaarrhhhhhhh" that lived stifled in my head.

I was in an unhappy marriage and struggling with a growing sense of disconnection. My unhappiness came to move in cycles that had peaks and valleys. When I became unable to stuff the way I felt down any longer, I packed up and left taking our daughter with me, leaving my husband to come home to an empty house. I was still in the program at Holyoake, and being strongly encouraged to stay on my own until I'd done enough recovery work to be clearer about who I was, and what I really wanted. It was vitally important before making any further choices or decisions about anything.

Nevertheless, not long after settling into a rented unit, I met a man through a friend and began a short-lived affair. It was most certainly not right for me and not something I even enjoyed. It was in fact, a futile attempt to leave my marriage behind and numb myself against the depth of fear, pain and loneliness I felt.

My husband threatened suicide, saying he'd drive himself at high speed into a tree. I would have to tell our child I was responsible for his death. He threatened to take our daughter from me, using my childhood as proof I was an unfit mother. When that didn't make me go running back, he arrived one night on my doorstep with his wrists cut, dripping blood in the doorway.

He broke in to my unit and went through my things while I wasn't at home, and harassed me on the phone. He'd come to pick up our daughter for access visits, and refuse to leave, staying to fight with me instead. At night he sometimes spied on me through my windows. One evening he even turned the power off in the meter box, plunging us into darkness in an attempt to regain control. When I put my head out the front window to demand he turn the power back on, he furiously took a swing at my head.

Another night he rang very late and demanded I come to him. He'd swallowed a box of Panadol tablets, washed down by half a bottle of neat Scotch. At the time our daughter was in bed sleeping. My choice was to leave her alone while I went to rescue him or wake her up and drag her along to witness the distress.

I phoned the local hospital and asked what the outcome was of taking so many Panadol with that much alcohol. I was told it could do serious damage to the vital organs of the body, even result in death. Angry with him for putting me in such a position, and knowing it was emotional blackmail, I rang his next-door neighbours and asked them to check on him and call an ambulance if one was needed.

I was gone for four months before I gave up my bid for what felt like self-preservation, returning like a beaten child needing to be taken care of.

After settling back in, I became worried about my daughter's behaviour. She'd become emotionally explosive and was not doing well at school. It had become common for her to have volatile meltdowns, particularly in the car after picking her up at the end of the day, often before I'd even left the school grounds. Many times she told me she hated school and wanted to kill herself.

I went to see a doctor I'd been advised was good medically, but also very tuned in and a good listener. During the appointment, my daughter sat on the floor playing frenetically with the toys in the middle of the room. As the doctor listened to my concerns, he watched her, looking intrigued. He asked if I'd ever heard of Attention Deficit Disorder, and when I said no, a brief explanation ensued. When I left, I walked out clutching a book on the subject, along with a referral to a Developmental Paediatrician.

The Specialist made the diagnoses quickly and easily, his manner detached and matter-of-fact. He then informed me about the medications used for treatment. I didn't know anything about the condition, so wanted to check into it further before putting my daughter on any kind of drug. I asked about additional investigations that could be done to back up the diagnosis, as well as other options for treatment. I wasn't convinced and didn't feel I knew enough to make an informed decision.

The Paediatrician reacted with poorly veiled impatience and annoyance at my questioning his authority and good judgment. However, he gave me the details of a Clinical Educational Psychologist he said would categorically back up his diagnosis. In his opinion, I was just wasting time and denying my daughter the treatment she needed.

At the Psychologists appointment, my daughter was put through a process of testing to rate her performance and intelligence. The results showed she was in the superior rage with her IQ, but she had considerable fear about getting things wrong. Her fear made her highly stressed and therefore slow at what she did, always second-guessing herself. He didn't think she had ADD at all. Maybe there were other things going on. His attention turned to me.

I was asked about my life in general, and about my childhood. His line of questioning made me uncomfortable and defensive. It was a road I was not going to go down, and I felt certain my childhood had nothing to do with my daughter. How could it? She hadn't been there, and she'd never seen or experienced the things I had. Ruffled, I left his rooms certain he didn't know what he was talking about.

Still not happy with the ADD diagnosis, I went to another specialist paediatrician for a second opinion. The first diagnosis was backed up without any further investigation or additional questioning.

I read the book I was given and bought a few others. The more I researched what ADD was, the more it seemed to fit, including the reasons why my daughter's brightness hadn't come through in the classroom. The script for medication was filled and she went on it.

The books also said ADD was a hereditary disorder and predominantly a male problem. I looked to my husband and realised he had many of the attributes fitting Adult ADD. He'd also struggled at school as a child, but I also recognised much of it explained my own way of being, and failure to learn at school.

I became a keen advocate of the condition and quite the expert on the subject, even starting a support group in our area with two other women. The ADD issue took up a lot of my focus and attention over the following years. In my ignorance, it was a great deflection from where I really needed to go, to find and free the truth.

My husband decided to buy a plastics fabrication company. I wasn't keen on the idea. I didn't think we needed the risk or the burden, but my husband had already made up his mind. A long-time friend of his was to be the manager, and I was asked to be the secretary, an even less appealing idea. If I was going to be allowed to work, I would have much preferred to do something in-line with discovering and pursuing my own aspirations. However, my husband was adamant he needed me to keep an eye on things. He wouldn't have the time. He was also insistent I be a silent partner in the company he was setting up to purchase the business, telling me it was for tax purposes only.

At first, the novelty of the situation did provide some enjoyment. I was learning new skills and feeling good about having a measure of responsibility. I oversaw the phone at the front office, the paying of wages and taking care of the accounts.

As time went by, I became aware we were getting into financial difficulty. The withholding tax from employees' wages was being spent to keep the business going, rather than being paid to the taxation department as it should have been.

Several times I expressed concern to my husband. I let him know I thought the manager was doing a poor job and saw his incompetence in pricing work as part of the problem. There were other things going on I didn't fully understand, but when I tried to find out more, I was blocked by both the manager and my husband.

Frustrated and worried, I continued to try to get my husband to investigate what was happening, but he dismissed my apprehensions entirely.

When I reminded him he'd sent me in as spy in the first place, so should at least consider my concerns, he refused to talk about it at all.

At work, I spent most of my time on the phone trying to get debtors to pay their overdue accounts, so we could pay ours. We ran on a bank over-draft that always needed to be extended just to cover wages. With no money to spare, the withholding tax debt continued to grow. I became a nervous wreck and sores broke out on my scalp. Unable to take it any longer, I quit.

My life and my choices were full of contradictions. I tried so very hard to accept my marriage, and I tried to live in it as best I could, the way I saw other people doing. Part of that for me was the blind desire to grow my family. In the in-between moments of what was for me, normalcy, I wanted another child. I had a disquieting hollowness that needed to be filled, and I thought having a new baby to look forward to and prepare for, was what I needed.

I underwent micro-surgery to reconnect the remnants of the Fallopian tube on my right side. Enough had been saved from my last ectopic pregnancy, to make another attempt at conceiving naturally, worth a try. It failed, and I had a third ectopic episode. It was a dismal experience.

When the pregnancy was first confirmed, my doctor needed to continue monitoring my hormone levels to track the pregnancies' viability. They were low, signifying there may be a problem. I already feared the baby was growing in the wrong place. I was having a lot of familiar pain and discomfort. More blood tests were done over the ensuing weeks, and I waited fretfully by the phone for each result, until finally, my doctor advised my pregnancy was not viable. When the call came, I was instructed to get myself to the hospital immediately. Arrangements had already been made for my admission, and I would be prepped for surgery that afternoon.

After the phone call with my doctor, I went in search of my husband, ashen-faced and afraid. He was in the front garden mixing cement in his wheelbarrow. Tearfully, I explained the situation and asked him to take me to the hospital right away. He stood straight-backed, looked at the trowel in his hand, then back down at the barrow and said, "What the bloody hell am I supposed to do with this lot then?" He was more emotionally responsive to the idea of losing a fresh barrow of cement, than the real risk I faced.

I healed, picked up and plodded on. My husband and I were going through one of our 'good' patches and I'd become addicted to aerobics. The adrenaline rush from working my body gave me a sense of power and freedom. At crest moments during a work-out, I felt my body and my spirit soar.

I still longed for another child. In Vitro Fertilisation was now my only option. During my second cycle of treatment, I was unexpectedly picked to compete in an amateur aerobics competition. If I was to win, I'd have the opportunity to compete in Melbourne. If I won there, I could move up into professional competition.

In the beginning, I'd had it in mind that if the IVF failed after a reasonable number of attempts, I'd have my aerobics to fall back on. I would go on to become an instructor. Trouble was, I was picked right at the time of egg harvest for the second cycle. If I chose the competition, I would have to forgo the cycle, ovulate and lose the eggs.

I really wanted to compete. I'd started experiencing a sense of personal pride and optimism about the possibility of accomplishing something outside my marriage, in turn reducing my desire to have another child. When I told my husband, he was angry. As far as he was concerned I had to finish the cycle. He didn't want me doing anything that threatened to grow me outside of my role as his wife in any way. I gave myself over to the IVF.

Once the decision had been made I forgot about myself and became re-involved in the hope of another child. The first time he came to the hospital to provide his sperm to fertilise my eggs, I felt a rush of warmth towards him. I saw it as a loving and generous act.

I had three fertilised eggs implanted and played the anxious waiting game that is so much a part of IVF treatment. When the news came I was pregnant, I was overjoyed, but I was advised not to get too excited.

Falling pregnant on the IVF program doesn't always mean taking a baby home in a basket. Regardless, I couldn't contain my joy, or my tears of gratitude and happiness. All thoughts of aerobics vanished.

At twelve weeks I started spotting and was referred for an ultrasound examination. During the exam, I waited anxiously, giving the radiographer time to locate the foetus and put together his findings. On the screen he pointed out my baby's heartbeat, and unexpectedly, a second. I was carrying twins.

Nothing could have prepared me for the fear I felt about losing my babies after suffering so many previous disappointments. I read everything I could about multiple pregnancies, and as the weeks passed and my belly grew, so did a feeling of uneasiness. Something bad was going to happen. Something bad always happened. I was steeling myself against it, trying to force it not to happen.

At twenty weeks, I had a second ultrasound and discovered I was carrying boys. I hadn't even considered I could be having sons. The wholehearted excitement I felt, took me by surprise. I considered I must have come a long way in overcoming my aversion to the idea of birthing and breast feeding a male.

The good patch in my marriage came to an end and the same old squabbles returned. My husband and I fought a lot over our daughter. He was often giving her a tough time, and I was constantly trying to make it up to her by being too lenient, guilty, sad and regretful.

I became so tense my jaw locked, and I couldn't chew food. I felt vulnerable and unsafe at every turn. At twenty-three weeks, I started having premature contractions, and was admitted to the labour ward of our local hospital. It was such a relief to be taken out of home and cocooned in a safe place. I'd be taken care of and my babies monitored. I didn't even worry about my daughter. I just needed to hide and hold my babies safe.

Under strict instructions to remain horizontal, I lay in bed for seven weeks before the contractions started again. I became four centimetres dilated. An ambulance was organised, and I was rushed to King Edward Memorial Hospital. The birth was expected to be imminent.

To everyone's astonishment, I didn't go into full labour. Rather, I lingered in limbo, stressed by my long confinement, and frazzled by physical discomfort and prolonged uncertainty.

As the weeks ticked by, I became keenly attuned to my babies. I knew the baby on the bottom was fine. He was in the right position, head engaged, and very active. The second baby however, lay transverse on top, and barely moved at all. Something told me he was in danger. I started to nag the nursing staff to do checks on his heart with the heart monitor, but each time, all appeared well. A few days went by and my feeling of foreboding became so acute, I started to panic. I just knew something was wrong. I'd felt no movement whatsoever from him for quite some time. I nagged continually until the nurse assigned to me gave in and agreed to do another heart rate check.

I watched the monitor and listened to the familiar, reassuring sounds of the bottom baby as his heart pumped rhythmically. Then the nurse turned her attention to the top baby. There was hardly any heart rhythm at all. He was bordering on flat-lining.

That afternoon my sons were born by emergency caesarean. The placenta had died, causing the stronger twin on the bottom to use his brother as his replacement food supply, and drain him of most of his blood. Within hours of the births, the weaker twin, who was severely anaemic, developed pneumonia that was resistant to most of the antibiotics tried. I didn't know if he was going to live or die. It was a difficult, exhausting and frightening time.

I remained in hospital for a week before being discharged, but my babies stayed behind until they were strong enough to come home. I began my daily sojourns to the hospital to establish breast-feeding and deliver bottles of expressed breast milk.

Being flat on my back for three months after being so active, had taken its toll on my body. I'd put on over twenty kilos and lost only four after my babies were born. My back had weakened considerably, and I felt ungainly and bloated.

The boys came home after a month and it was the middle of winter. I lived with them in the family room to be close to the wood fire and slept on the sofa. It was hard to cope with the insecurity of being on my own with the twins after they'd been so well protected and watched over by nursing staff.

With the arrival of premature twin, the cracks in my marriage broke wide open. My extended stay in hospital had created a distance between my husband and I that bordered on us being strangers. There was little eye contact and no physical closeness or affection of any kind.

Again I experienced motherhood as a bungled effort. My babies were tiny and seemed so fragile, and fully breast feeding both was an enormous undertaking. They never slept for longer than a few minutes at a time, and when they cried it was always together. I never knew which one to pick up first.

Each day was spent running on nervous energy. My daughter had trouble accepting her new brothers. She'd had no mother while I was gone and when I returned, I was still gone. The twins took everything I had.

Things about my life I'd previously taken for granted disappeared, every small freedom, which in this situation were shown to be big freedoms unappreciated. I didn't have one moment where I could complete anything undisturbed, not take a shower, clean the bathroom, or cook a meal. I failed daily in what I thought I was supposed to be able to accomplish as a housewife and mother, and I lost the companionship of my one and only female friend. Her withdrawal was a deeply felt loss. She was the closest thing I'd ever experienced to emotionally bonded sisterhood, something I didn't have with my biological sisters. I truly loved her.

Growing angry and frustrated, I asked for support from my husband, both physical and emotional. I needed his help, but he added to my feelings of inadequacy by retorting with, "Anybody would think you were the only woman to have ever had twins." We fought constantly, just as the twins cried constantly. I had only one pair of arms and spent many nights over long hours pacing the lounge room floor trying to comfort each in turn.

Both babies became very sick with a dreadful cold. Their coughing was so sticky and prolonged it seemed they couldn't take another breath. When they reached what would have been their forty-week gestation period, one twin developed a testicular hernia and was rushed to Princess Margaret hospital. The other followed suit with the same condition in the emergency room while his brother was being tended to. Both boys were given pethidine to relieve their unbearable agony. During surgery to correct the problem, the twin who'd nearly died from pneumonia, nearly died on the operating table. His heart had stopped beating.

Winter was thankfully coming to an end, and the sun shone more often through our large, family room window. I didn't think it necessary to have the twins so protectively rugged up all the time, so I let them lay together in their bassinet, jumpsuits on but no blanket or beanie, thinking they'd be warmed by the heat coming through the window. Feeding time came and neither baby woke, so I tried to rouse them. The little one, who'd already had such a struggle to survive, was white, listless and unable to be woken. After rushing him to the children's hospital we discovered his temperature had dropped life-threateningly low. I hadn't known that underweight babies were not able to retain their body heat on their own.

By the time the twins were three months old, they'd put on enough much needed heat sustaining weight, for me to feel secure about leaving the protective warmth of the lounge room. I desperately wanted to get back into my own bed. But it was a fight to get there. My husband was disinterested in me, and even though two, brand new white cots had been set up in our bedroom for some time, he did not want the inconvenient disturbance of our babies in them.

Chapter 7

THE SEARCH

MANY times during troubled years, I wondered what it would feel like to rest with my sense of brokenness healed. I sometimes imagined in my mind, the large, benevolent, fatherly hand of God reaching down and scooping me up. I would see my body drop into His palm while letting out a deeply held sigh, knowing I would no longer need to push myself to keep going.

A powerful yet soothing voice would tell me the war was over. It would say, "Come and rest in me my child, there will be no more pain or suffering." But as hard as I wished, as hard as I prayed, the hand never came. My imaginings only ever served to make the longing more intense, leaving me with a deep, aching sadness at being so alone.

Sometimes I prayed for mercy, never believing I would ever be worthy of it. I carried a burden of profound guilt. In my early twenties, there'd been times when I attempted to look for God in religion, cautiously disguising myself among the different church congregations of the small towns I lived in, praying they wouldn't discover me as an imposter in their midst.

But my search for God never came from the heart with an open eagerness to find the light of love; it came from gripping fear and the deep desire for absolution over being such a bad human being. I was driven by a need to receive His pardon, without which I would be forever hiding in fear and shadows. It was a search I'd given up, until, as a woman in my thirties with a husband and three children, I began my crying, my yearning, all over again.

I could not understand why the issue of God was a recurring unease hanging over me. I felt a tired longing, an insatiable craving for safety and rest, and knew it was tied up with my murky history.

Just where did God fit into all this anyway, and if He were real, where was He? Did He purposely allow bad things to happen to bad people, simply turning His back because they were not worthy of His noticing? It seemed the light of His love never shone on me. He never answered my prayers.

My life had become a shattered existence and I needed to discover the logic behind the madness of its demise. Was there a designed purpose for it, a gift or lesson to be found among the shards scattered round? And if so, was it worth the heartache involved in trying to retrieve the broken and strewn pieces. I had so many unanswered questions that left me feeling fractured in my mind and the very depths of my soul.

In the end I discovered I had to be willing to come out from my hiding place, willing to question all the beliefs I had ever had about myself, my life, my family, and everything I'd been taught about the nature of God. I had to grow the courage to expose the truth, hidden in amongst the tangled web of lies keeping me from the peace I craved.

As a pilgrim for wholeness I walked further into the labyrinth of my history. I began my quest as the fool, stepping naively over the edge of a cliff, only to descend deep into the shadow-lands. I crawled on my hands and knees in the darkness and dragged myself through slime; the sum of every dirty and shameful thing ever done to me. Every loveless look and touch, every scary demon of the darkness, and every bad thing I had ever done, thought or said. I slowly fell apart. Finally, my inconsolable longing, pain, and unanswered questions, led me into the deepest, blackest depression I've ever known.

I had no idea what was to unfold when I first began to question my life, let alone how it would end. If I had, I don't think I would have had the courage to go through it. Life itself conspired to heal me, sometimes leading me in a dance filled with shapeless shadows that haunted me for what seemed like an eternity. The more I delved into my past, the more in touch with my feelings of badness I became. Judgement was etched into my soul, something I accepted as an inescapable truth.

Adding to my burden, I carried a great deal of accumulated hurt, bitterness and resentment from my marriage. I'd changed as a person over the years and had become combative and punitive in my own behaviour. The squirming agitation and dissatisfaction I lived with sometimes drove me to unstable mood swings and bouts of self-righteous antagonism.

But there were also times in-between when I was determined to work through it. I wanted a happy, normal family life, and I wanted to be able to change the way I felt so I could love my husband and be content. Except something inside me wouldn't be satisfied.

Sessions with a progression of conventional mental health-care professionals served only to deepen a growing sense of blindness. I was diagnosed as having a major depressive illness, as well as the possibility of Adult Attention Deficit Disorder. Furthermore, I was told I would probably need medication for the rest of my life. I was put on anti-depressants and Dexamphetamine. It was to be some time before I received the correct diagnosis of Complex Post Traumatic Stress Disorder.

The pills literally kept me functioning. However, with the strain of a disastrous marriage, trying to care for my daughter and the taxing addition of twins, I became increasingly suppressed and despondent.

Episodes of a painful swelling in my throat became frequent and intense, often waking me in the night from dreams filled with unspeakable grief. Something I didn't have words for, was trying to find its way to the surface. I got steadily worse, not better.

A growing exhaustion resulted in half done jobs around the house. Standing at the kitchen sink long enough to finish the dishes was almost impossible. I'd put washing on but couldn't follow through with hanging it out right away. It usually sat in the basket until the next day. I was always disorganised, and dinner was frequently late.

Investigating the New Age movement gave me hope in finding something to fill my emptiness. The God I'd been raised with was not going to help me. My beliefs told me I wasn't worthy of His approval. I did not want to upset Him by coming out from under my rock, contaminating what was clean. As long as I remained hidden, He would never know I was there. My hiding place kept me safe from His vengeance.

I was vulnerable to concepts that, on the surface, seemed to offer me a haven. Some of the New Age beliefs, like abuse as karma for perpetrating the same kind of abuse on a child in a past life, or the belief that abuse happens as a planned spiritual lesson for the development of the human soul, gave what appeared to be a plausible explanation. Everything that happens to us is perfect in a perfect universe. All is as it should be in the divine order of things, all serving for our growth and greater good.

If these concepts were true it really was very simple. I was learning what it felt like to be on the receiving end of what I'd done to another, while gaining experience to develop my soul. Reincarnation gave me the opportunity to make amends for my previous life's misdeeds, while adding to my spiritual growth.

These explanations fitted in nicely with my low self-image and belief I deserved to be punished. After all, I was a sinful creature. They served to perpetuate entrenched feelings of being fundamentally polluted, but at the same time were enticing in their offer of redemption through the cycle of rebirth.

If I could redeem myself by being good and accept my childhood as divine justice, there would be no need for anger, no need to struggle against it. Yet even as I tried to make these ideas fit, something inside me screamed with rage and revulsion. I felt tired from the burden I was carrying and had reached the point of wanting to die and stay dead. For me the idea of reincarnation was a torment I couldn't come to terms with.

If God created this kind of teaching method for his children to learn and evolve spiritually, then I hated Him. What kind of sinister God was capable of causing and endorsing such horrendous pain in the name of love? It was no different to the 'love' my father gave me when he beat me for being bad.

I didn't realise I was sinking further into the slime, or how much further I was actually moving away from God. Who was I to question the wisdom of God and the divine order of the universe anyway?

I gathered information from whatever crossed my path, discarding what didn't seem to fill in the gaps with an explanation, and putting together what did like a badly constructed jigsaw puzzle. I longed to find something in me that was redeemable.

I turned to crystals, Tarot cards, and astrology in my search for answers. The world of fairy folk, nymphs and nature spirits, seemed a lot more appealing than what I was running from. Ignorant, I dabbled in things capable of causing enormous harm to someone who is filled with dark imaginings and carrying religious baggage. These practices, as far as I'd been taught, came under the heading of occultism and were the realm of Satan.

Christian people began popping up out of nowhere; stirring my qualms with warnings about how dangerous it was to be playing with fire. Repeatedly I was warned it was the way of the devil and my soul was in danger. The more I was warned the more my qualms grew. I rationalised their appearance was because God Himself was trying to scare me into obedience, but I'd become so angry and disillusioned with God, it made me all the more determined.

I felt beneath these good and pious people. They had a relationship with God, understood his ways and were close to Him. The truth was I'd spent most of my life running from the clutches of the devil and the wrath of God and trying to hide it. The black stuff inside me, the hidden evil, was my secret alone. I'd worked hard to keep it buried just to have a life. I'd shielded myself so well behind the mask I wore, even I'd forgotten. But now the mask was slipping, and I couldn't stand the thought that after all this time; someone might now discover the truth.

The concern and good intentions for the welfare of my soul served only to re-ignite an obscured terror of the devil, reminding me of his presence cast over my childhood. I feared I was in fact one of his children. If I wasn't a part of God's kingdom, there was nowhere else to go.

In my peripheral vision I began to see black-hooded figures around my house. I was on the run again. Memories of the dark and being very afraid resurfaced, promising reckoning. It was breathing down my neck. Thoughts of the devil and demons became more intrusive.

When I used my crystals and Tarot cards, or read my astrology books, I felt him getting closer. I tried to ignore the heaviness around me, the shadows closing in. I didn't want to give in to the sweetness of the good people. They made me sick with their sanctimonious warnings and scare-tactic Bible-bashing. The dark part of me hidden in the shadows hated the way they seemed so perfect.

I bought a large five-pointed quartz crystal at a New Age festival, chosen to symbolise my husband, our three children and myself. Each point was uncannily perfect in its representative proportions. I didn't understand much about them at the time but was interested to learn. I read books on their different uses, how to cleanse with them, meditate with them, and meet nature spirits through them. I had it in mind to purify myself and my home through the power the crystal contained.

I would hold it up to the light, look deeply into its reflected colours and angles, and imagine an unseen world looking back at me. I fantasised about developing psychic abilities and being able to communicate with that world. As eager as I was to use my new crystal, I still fostered fearful thoughts about evil and the devil, worried he was going to appear any moment and take my soul to hell.

Soon after buying the crystal, I decided to sleep with it under my pillow. I had read it could increase my powers of perception and help me to have prophetic dreams. But when I lay my head on the pillow and closed my eyes, I immediately saw a spiralling, dark whirlpool of hieroglyphics that sucked my consciousness down into blackness. I passed out. It's the last thing I remember before waking early hours in the morning, with my bedside lamp on and my naked body strewn across the bed.

My arms were rigid above my head with my hands joined together at the wrist, as if tied by an invisible cord. My bottom was on the very edge of the bed, legs spread apart with my feet on the floor. Alarmed, I sat up and looked around the room, trying to grasp what had happened. A dense, spiky cold fear prickled my skin.

I looked over at my husband and saw he was in an unusually deep sleep, in the same position he'd been in when I'd first come to bed. As a rule, he was a very light sleeper. I couldn't believe he hadn't woken during all the movement that must have taken place.

Something out of the ordinary had happened. I pulled my nightdress back over my head, put the crystal in the drawer of my bedside table and turned out the light. Sliding beneath the covers, I cowered with my head under my pillow frozen with fright, just as I'd done so many times as a child.

Not long after that incident the crystal broke, splitting in half in my hands. There were three points, one large and two small on one half, and one large and one small, on the other. Given the crystal and its five points were symbolic of my family and myself, I took it as a bad sign.

Life became additionally oppressive, the atmosphere in my home thickened and my ability to manage degenerated further. I felt strangely unreal. Slowly I crumbled, becoming paranoid and frightened, saturated in negativity and fear. But I kept looking, kept dabbling, until there were just too many scary things happening.

Believing I'd gone too far and the devil was at hand, I gathered my books and crystals into a bag ready to take to the tip, and burned my Tarot cards in the family room fireplace. As I watched them burn hot and bright, I imagined I was burning the devil, too.

I also had home-blended face creams containing essential oils my friend and I had made prior to my pregnancy. We'd used a crystal to divine which oils were the right ones for my emotional and spiritual needs, and since coming home from the hospital, I'd been using them daily. Over the weeks, as my fears intensified, my face felt as though it was gradually changing. It was a strange sensation, as though my cell structure was altering underneath the surface of my skin. I gathered up the creams and put them into the bag ear-marked for the rubbish tip.

I tried to dig into myself, searching for a reasonable explanation as to why I was so filled with fear of evil and the devil, matched only by an equally deep fear of God. I came to a blank, impassable wall. The only thing I could come up with, was that it must have stemmed from the early negative influences of religion in my childhood.

As a child I was raised with Catholic teachings, though my parents were not practicing Catholics. My father had been while growing up, until something happened that made him turn away from the faith he'd been raised with. My grandparents were very strong Catholics, of the fire and brimstone variety, especially my grandmother. She pulled me up for every known misdemeanour in my use of language, behaviour and etiquette, citing each transgression as a sin. If I ate too much, told a lie or was disrespectful, I was speedily reminded about going to hell. God was always watching with a score pad, keeping tabs on every mistake I made.

I was told I needed to pray and go to church. It had to be the Catholic Church of course because that was the only true religion; all others were outside the truth of God and the kingship of Jesus. To me the Church was as ominous and as threatening as the devil. My life was already frightening enough, so where could I go? There was no love or safety anywhere.

No one knew what I lived with as a child, or what I was dealing with in my adult life. I was going silently crazy on my own with a secret world inside my head. I learned well at an early age how to conceal things so my outside was never a true reflection of what was going on inside me. I always felt alone, lost in a vast, dark and barren land, unable to connect to anyone. Nothing existed within me, only a thick and heavy dullness, devoid of any joy.

I lived with muted cries as the background to my thoughts, echoes from another time and place. Stuffing them down I'd try harder to play my role as wife and mother, unaware that for much of the time, I still lived in a semi-state of shock.

I became progressively ungrounded, unable to find anything to hold on to. The gulf between my husband and I widened still further as I avoided being available for sex. He became angrier at my rejection and lack of interest, and more volatile and intolerant of our children, taking his frustrations out on them. I couldn't stand it and again wanted to leave.

My husband must have sensed I was getting ready to run. In desperation he came home one night with a cutting from a newspaper. It was a story about a woman by the name of Dr Shirley Smith. She was the facilitator of a three-day Family of Origin Intensive dealing with healing relationships, and was running a series of evening talks that led into the program. My husband suggested we attend one.

The information night had an enormous impact on me, speaking to me in a language I easily understood. I was able to relate fully to what was being said, as though the steps I'd already taken to heal myself were the groundwork for just this very experience. Everything struck a deep cord.

I knew the program was something I had to be involved in. My husband wanted to be a part of it with me, but it was made clear from the outset by the people running the seminar he had to participate with his focus on himself, not me. He assigned ninety percent of the blame for the problems in our marriage to me, and gave himself only ten percent, so in his thinking if I was fixed, all would be well.

As much as I knew I was not coping with my life and that I had issues to deal with, I also knew my husband had his own problems he was not prepared to face. I was not going to allow my childhood to be used against me. Putting the majority of the fault for our troubles at my door, was his way of not looking at himself, his own painful childhood, and how that impacted him and his ability to be in a relationship.

It was made clear whatever I got out of the seminar had to be my own experience, free from any influence from my husband. If our marriage was to survive, we each had to take responsibility for our own wounds, beliefs and behaviours. We each had to examine how our respective childhoods had affected us as individuals, and in turn, how it played out in our relationship. It meant being open to honest self-examination.

For me I had nothing to lose. I'd already left my marriage twice, returning the second time after six months under much the same circumstances as the first. I put off leaving my marriage for a third time, in the hope this program could heal the ache in my soul.

I had a deep urgency to save myself. I wanted to have a life free of the death I carried inside, unseen by anyone, and not understood by me. I knew conventional therapy couldn't help, only prop me up with medication and labels. I also knew the pain came from another place, but I didn't know where that place was, or how to find it. As a seeker of freedom, I began a pilgrimage into my own interior.

On arrival for our first day in the workshop, I felt afraid. I'd been through such a terrible time fighting the devil and evil imaginings that I'd overloaded on fear. I knew the program was to include subtle hypnosis through the power of suggestion, meditation, music and visualisation techniques, and that it was spiritually-based in content.

All the warnings and previous conversations I'd had with the Christian people still echoed in my head. Even meditation was taboo unless it was done with a Christian Bible in hand; otherwise the devil would have an open gateway. Yet something inside I couldn't put my finger on, pushed me past my apprehension. The introduction evening had captured me with a beckoning ring of Truth.

The moment I set foot into the room, something began to release. I felt like a wounded, vulnerable child, eyes downcast in shame. I was no longer adult size, but small, wanting only to hide, yet desperate to be seen at the same time. Everyone else seemed to be experiencing something similar.

Tears flowed easily as the energy began to shape the process of the workshop. The atmosphere was alive and palpable. We were sheltered together in fellowship. Nothing existed outside of the room and the space specifically created for the express purpose of what I can only describe as, cleansing soul work.

At the beginning of the Intensive, we were instructed to set a clear intention for what we hoped to achieve. I set my intention at freedom. I had no clear idea what I meant by that, or what it would look like when I found it. It was such a desperate feeling. Soon enough it became clear it was freedom from the past, freedom from the confines of my mind, and freedom from the black shadows that had been my constant companions for as long as I could remember.

My husband and I remained on opposite sides of the room so we could be uninhibited by each other's presence. During the program we only came together for specific processes requiring us being together as a couple.

We talked little to each other as the three and a half days progressed. I was coming face to face with myself at a level I never expected, connecting with subterranean parts. In a mirror exercise, I physically experienced how much I hated myself, discovering the meaning of toxic shame. My stomach muscles tightened and twisted in painful spasms as I tried to look at my own reflection. Waves of nausea rose and fell as I grappled to hold my own gaze.

I saw cloudy grey smog surrounding my body. I understood it was my energy field, the filter through which I experienced the world, and through which people experienced me. It was oppressive and gloomy.

During an exercise in grief work, I found myself in a cavernous depth of sorrow I could have drowned in, crying tears unlike any tears I'd ever cried before, the sound raw and ravaged to my ears. These were the wailings of my soul, the tears I never cried as a child when all I could do was curl up, shut down and disappear.

For much of the time my body ached, my head hurt, and the vibration from the sound of my own voice caused unbearable throbbing. Determined, I pushed through, wanting to get everything out of it I could. I was captivated by the process of learning, welcoming of the tears and the pain. I desperately wanted to heal.

As difficult as it was, my participation in the Intensive became the anchor I'd been searching for. It acted as the catalyst for my spiritual awakening, building a fragile but tangible bridge between the world of light, and my world of shadows. I received a miracle, a vision in answer to a heart-felt prayer.

Late in the afternoon on the last day, we were going through a guided Inner Child meditation and I was filled with trepidation. I'd never been able to connect to myself as a child. I thought that part of me was dead. I knew it was vital for me to find her if I was going to make it through the rest of my life.

As we were being led through the process of the meditation, I started to panic. All I could see was the same familiar dark and empty void. I longed to see my inner child and time was running out, the meditation would soon be over. I kept trying to force, with the strength of my own will, some kind of contact. But the more I tried to force it, the more hopeless I felt.

Dr Smith had already talked to us about the concept of a Higher Power and had instructed us to use that term if we weren't comfortable with the word God. She was herself an ordained minister, but there was no pressure to see God in any particular way, or to associate God with any particular belief system. It was an open invitation to approach God in whatever way felt safe and comfortable for us. If at any time we found ourselves struggling with the meditations, or any other part of the program, all we had to do was ask for help from that higher source.

I'd asked for God's help many times over the years, with what I thought was no response. He either did not hear me or just didn't care. But it was here at the Family of Origin workshop I finally found His presence.

Abruptly I let go of trying and released my will from force. My body went limp as I surrendered the struggle. I could not do anything on my own. Remembering the instruction of the workshop leader, I opened my heart and asked my Higher Power for help. Unexpectedly, and within an instant of the request being made, a breathtaking image replaced the familiar, desolate black.

A young girl lay on green grass with her arms neatly by her sides. She looked like a sleeping princess from some long-forgotten fairytale. There were no flowers or birds, no animals or butterflies, not even a whisper of a breeze, only tranquil stillness. Though there was no obvious movement, there was an aliveness flickering in the atmosphere, as though the particles of golden light from the sun were alive.

The girl's body rested alongside the edge of a motionless, crystal clear creek. I put her at age six, an assumption made because of the age I'd been when my uncle came to my bed. Confusingly, it didn't quite fit. She looked older. Quickly I put my confusion aside, preferring instead to just look at her. What I was seeing was incredible.

The little girl wore a simple white satin dress that came to the knee, with a band of white satin ribbon around her waist. White stockings covered her legs, white shoes rested on her feet, and a white satin bow sparkled against the glossy darkness of her hair. She was in the middle of a large clearing, protected and encircled by a grove of giant trees. The sun streamed down its shimmering rays, covering her in a blanket of warmth, which seemed also to be her source of nourishment.

The child was my essence, the essential part of my Self that had fled from the harshness of my life. I literally felt the glowing warmth of the sun from my vision spread throughout my body as I lay in meditation on the carpeted floor. It was as though the sun were inside the centre of me, fanning outwards. I realised she was inside me, but somewhere else at the same time.

I could still hear what was happening in the room and the voice leading the meditation. Dr Smith was now instructing us to invite our inner child to take our hand and merge into us. The intention was to bring about integration and a sense of wholeness. In exchange we were to make an offering by being willing to give something up. I chose to give up my toxic shame.

I called to the child and stretched out my hand. There was no response. I called again but still she didn't move. Her eyes remained closed tight and her body deathly still. Realising she wasn't breathing, I stared disbelievingly, closely watching her chest for any signs of movement. There was nothing. My heart shattered. Internally, it felt like I was caving in on myself.

It seemed the most important part of me really was dead. Stricken, I tried to comprehend what was happening. I was so close to her, yet I may as well have been a million miles away. She didn't know I was there.

I had come so far, dragged my body along in search of life and found only death. How could I continue to live without her? She was my innocence and laughter, my giggles and wonder at the beauty of life. She was my positive creativity and imagination, my trust and ability to love.

The meditation ended. We were bought back to the present and I was in a state of shock. I felt as though my soul was gone. I couldn't speak, and my body was trembling.

We were instructed to have a tea break and to talk to no one, keeping quiet within ourselves until after the break was over. Only then could we debrief in our small groups.

Shaking uncontrollably, I walked outside and stood on the footpath, leaning against the wall of the building for support. Another woman, a participant in the workshop, saw I was struggling with something and approached, but as she went to open her mouth to speak, I gestured for her to move away. I couldn't bear to be with anyone other than myself and the experience I was having.

It was the middle of a sunny Sunday afternoon. Cars were whizzing by and people were going about their business on the city streets. Feeling frighteningly disconnected, I stared at my surroundings and tried to comprehend what had just happened.

I was teetering on the edge of what felt like possible oblivion, not knowing if I was going to slip over it into madness. My eyes searched the sky, looking for the light and warmth of the sun. I felt cold inside. I looked at the trees and buildings around me, noticing everything seemed drained of colour. Nothing was real anymore. It was too much to cope with alone. Silently I called to God, asking to understand what the vision had meant. Instantly I received an answer.

A male voice spoke in my mind, saying "Do not be afraid. She is not dead, only sleeping. All you have to do is go to her, hold her in your arms and breathe your breath back into her."

In those moments of precious communication, I had no surroundings, no body that I was aware of. Time itself had ceased to exist, allowing a door to be opened through which I could be reached. When I again realised I was on the footpath, everything I looked at had a brightness of colour and vivid life. The world around me appeared new, as though I were seeing it for the first time.

Feelings of peace and joy flooded through me. I'd received a gift undreamed of. I had the certainty, for the first time in my life, that I was not alone. How could this happen to someone like me? God did not spit on me, He did not throw lightning bolts at me and there was no furious gnashing of teeth. There was no hint of judgment toward me whatsoever, not for anything I have ever done in my life I've judged to be wrong, not for mistakes I've made, nor things I've been ashamed of doing as a result of my history. All I felt was support and encouragement in my endeavour to find my way home.

The image I'd been raised with was a lie. I didn't need to hide anymore. I knew I was safe and supported in my journey through this life, and my continued healing. I understood an unseen hand was with me and had been all along, bringing me slowly to the dawning of freedom, and at a pace I could handle.

So many times I'd prayed and found no comfort, only a deeper sense of loneliness. I had always felt isolated and estranged from the rest of the human race. But now my loneliness and isolation had become connection, my fear and despair, joy.

Nothing of my essential self was destroyed or made dirty by acts done to me against my will. I was not an evil, vile thing, blackened like tar on the inside as I'd secretly believed as a child. I now knew that part of me was held in a place of safety, not abandoned as I had always thought.

She was in fact, waiting for me to come and find her, to breathe her back to life.

The vision I was given in the Family of Origin seminar saved my life. I needed to know I was real, that I was salvageable. I needed to know there was still some part of me left that was good and clean. Nonetheless, it was only the beginning of yet another new phase of growth.

After the seminar nothing was the same. I looked at everything differently, my children, my marriage, who I was and what I wanted from life. Feelings of stillness hung over me as I was again suspended, trying to grasp all I'd dragged out of myself. I felt bewildered, not knowing how it would affect the rest of my life.

A door in my mind had been opened and I'd walked through it. I couldn't go back. I had gained a greater understanding of co-dependence, addiction, how we take on the roles and beliefs of others, and a better understanding of myself, yet there was still so much more to learn.

Over the years I'd often woken from sleep, gagging on wordless grief from intensely sorrowful dreams. The themes were always the same, rejection of me in some form by my parents. The nightmares happened intermittently, but increased dramatically during the tug-of-war years in my marriage.

One night in the first week following the program, I again woke choking on tears. The dream had been the worst ever. I fully felt the grief of my inner, unloved child, but this time, with the dream came complete comprehension of why my parents could never be there for me as a child, and why they were unable to be there for me still. I felt it and understood it at a level where language is inadequate and unnecessary. They had not loved the child, because they were not able to love her.

I took a special photo of myself as a little girl and went into the lounge room. Curled on the couch with a blanket, I grieved the loss, the pain and sorrow, for her and myself. I talked with her, stroked her and cuddled her. We lay there together for the longest time, embracing each other, until eventually sleep gave us both a place to rest, inside the warmth of each other. I have never had those dreams since. That part of me was healed.

Chapter 8

KALEIDOSCOPE

Hard won insights began the fashioning of a new person. I was in a struggle to find my own authenticity. Previously, I'd been the chameleon, changing to suit my environment in order to hide or survive.

Not much of the process was pleasurable. Most of it was excruciatingly exhausting, physically, psychologically and spiritually. Beginning with the Family of Origin seminar, I took the risk of looking inside myself to see if I was still alive, and uncovered many things about me and my life I'd been blind to.

I discovered what toxic shame was and the degree to which I carried it. It was venom that had struck to the very core of my being, saturating every cell in my body with its poison. I was filled with self-hatred and self-rejection. Everything about me was built on that foundation.

I realised the extent of how lost I'd been and for how long. The truth is my body had grown, but without much of me in it. I was not just hiding, but literally frozen somewhere in another place and time, somewhere my body couldn't go.

The only thing holding me now was Spirit. Not in a religious sense; but Spirit in a profoundly personal sense, in such a way that once I'd experienced it I could never turn my back to it. To do so would be a choice to remain forever in the dark. I knew I would never return to where I had been, could never deny something had changed inside me. My only option was to keep pushing forward.

The Family of Origin seminar had acted as a light switch, illuminating what had been hidden for so long. Where there had been darkness, daylight broke through, and with the light came the new possibility that I was a free being and loved by God. I came away with my blindfold removed. I now knew something extraordinary did in fact exist, and it was there for me as much as it was for everyone else.

I had always wanted to believe in God, but it had been a hope largely motivated by fear. I'd been too scared not to believe in him. He was the big Father riding on the clouds above, judging us, punishing us, and handing us over to the other side if we turned out to be the chaff and not the wheat.

It was never true. The spiritual world was in fact a compassionate and knowing realm, not the terrifying place of reckoning I'd been taught about as a child.

Emotionally I had to find room inside myself to accommodate the dawning Truth that I was acceptable and divine in origin. I realised I was already forgiven my flaws as a human being. Forgiveness had been mine before I was even born. My faults and failings were a non-issue in the spiritual realm because they were an accepted and expected part of any human journey. In the physical world however, forgiveness has a very important purpose with many aspects to it. Learning to forgive generates love, develops humility and compassion, while also being a doorway to personal growth and freedom.

I kept quiet about my vision and the voice I'd heard at the seminar. I needed time to process it. I never doubted the reality of what had happened, never doubted where it had come from, but I couldn't understand how I, of all people, had been graced with such an experience. It was a secret between God and me, a lifeline to seize hold of, but I also feared ridicule and criticism from my family if I started talking openly about such things, particularly from my father.

I couldn't tell my husband either. We didn't have the kind of safe, trusting relationship needed to discuss such things. He was closed when it came to spiritual or religious issues. But I also recognised I didn't want to share this with him. It was far too precious and personal, something I wanted to hold close.

I felt I had no right to be talking about spiritual matters anyway. I was a person with a sordid background. Spiritual phenomena were, to my understanding, reserved only for the heroes of religious history, not a shadow person like me. Believing this kept me constantly astounded and shame worked hard to convince me I was crazy. I couldn't fathom the love and mercy I'd been shown. Miraculously though, my terror and humiliation before God, slowly began changing into the first steps of petrifying trust.

There were times when I thought my experience of the Family of Origin seminar was more curse than blessing. It gave me the gift of knowing I was not alone, yet I struggled to put my life back together. I had no road map to show me the terrain I was travelling. At other times, I was in awe. I'd had a vision and been spoken to directly by spirit. Something huge had happened, and it had happened to me.

The problems in my marriage collided head-on with everything I was trying to comprehend about what I was experiencing. I couldn't deal with everything all at once. I had to keep re-adjusting and pulling myself back to the concerns of my family and the state of my relationship.

I tried to go on as normal. My husband and I planned a family day out at a fun park, but as we were driving along the busy highway toward our destination, I was overcome with a sudden, severe panic attack. It felt like something terrifying had ruptured in my chest and was trying to claw its way out. I couldn't breathe and tried to settle myself. I didn't want to fall apart. I didn't want the something to break through. Whatever it was, I wasn't ready for it. But the panic continued to rise.

The intensity of fear I felt was chilling. Any moment I was going to explode hysterically out of control. I had to get away from it. I turned my body toward the car door and gripped the handle, readying myself to jump out as we sped along the road. I knew I would be seriously hurt, maybe even killed if I flung myself out the door, but the overpowering terror I felt was far more dangerous. Silently I pleaded, "No, no, not here, please God, not now."

Immediately, the terror was gone. As suddenly as it had come, it had vanished. I let go of the door handle and settled myself back in my seat.

I ached inside to be reunited with the missing part of myself I'd seen in my meditation. Without her I was just an empty shell. I needed her to be whole, to be a loving partner, a good mother, and to make my life really work, not be split off and lost on some distant landscape in the unconscious or mystical world of spirit. This is where my body is. I wanted the rest of me here, too.

For the wounding of my spirit to be healed I had to breathe the breath of Life and raise the child. I needed to find the little girl I once was and love her back from the grave. Knowing she was real, waiting only for resurrection, made me realise it must be within my power to bring her back, but the voice I'd heard telling me I needed to restore myself, did not come with an instruction manual.

Although I'd had a spiritual breakthrough giving me a view of reality beyond what I'd always known, I had no experience in such things. I didn't know what it was supposed to achieve in me beyond what I'd initially received from it. While the seminar created a dilemma in one area, it set me free in another. I found myself hungry to know more of who and what God was. I became intent on a quest for knowledge and began a reading spree, poring over books on different spiritual beliefs and ideas. Like a starving kid in a lolly shop I ate my way through their many pages, taking in every word.

My intellect went into overdrive. Thinking and questioning became my tools to further loosen the straightjackets I had around my mind. In analysing, I tried to satisfy my wounded heart and sense of right and wrong. Some of what I read sent me packing right back into the arms of what I thought might be the devil. Bizarre ideas that conflicted outrageously with my ingrained and polarised religious understandings made my heart pound and my head spin. Other books felt safe and calming, nurturing and nourishing. I swung like a pendulum, moving back and forth between trying to hold onto my experience of spirit, and drowning in the sea of the un-known.

My hunger to explore was unexpected, by my husband and me. It took me further away from him. His hope had been that the workshop would ultimately help me come closer. He wanted our marriage to survive, but for me, nothing would ever be the same.

My childhood and adult life, my beliefs, emotions, dreams and illusions, had all been thrown up in the air together. Everything about who I thought I was had been dislodged from its previous place and was still in the process of falling, but nothing was going to land back to where it had been.

The seminar didn't just show me my shame, it didn't just provide a space for me to experience suppressed grief or confront my wounds, and it didn't just open a window to Spirit, it also revealed the foundation my marriage was built on.

I'd learnt about needy, dependant relationships. My husband and I were in one. I lacked a solid sense of self and was trying to suppress a lifetime of fear, insecurity and pain. I didn't know my husband as a separate person at any deep level and he didn't know me.

I also came to understand I had no idea what real love was, how to measure it in myself, or another person. As a couple my husband and I had a very shallow relationship, one that lacked healthy intimacy, sharing, connection, friendship, trust and communication.

My marriage was based on loneliness, neediness and sex. I had needed a life, a future. I wanted a home, a place I could be loved and cared for. I wanted to grow and be safe. My husband had his own issues he was running from, and his own needs, primarily met through sex. Sex gave, what was for him, love, reassurance and acceptance. It was a trade-off, not real love at all. We provided a place for each other to hide, to fend off the wolves that gnawed at our insides.

My husband and I mostly related to each other through fighting. It was how we avoided feeling our deepest feelings, or saying what really needed to be said, to ourselves as well as each other. We had make up sex followed by short periods of relative peace before the cycle our marriage moved in, started all over again. It had always been that way.

I had sex to gain acceptance, to avoid conflict, appease, comply and play my part. But now I was making a stand. I didn't want to have sex anymore out of duty. Doing it for the wrong reasons was dishonouring to my body as well as my soul. It served only to compound my feelings of resentment and anger. I wanted to experience being delighted in for who I was as a person. I wanted to be recognised and seen beyond my body, beyond my breasts and what I had between my legs.

I believed my husband and I could re-invent our relationship and build something new and healthy together. I could see myself easing back into a physical relationship in time, one that was both loving and giving, but I knew it could only happen if I was given the space I needed to develop into the person I was supposed to be.

I wanted to cultivate a fresh sense of trust, friendship and romance, without the pressure of having to have sex, and I needed his support and willingness to co-operate. Unable to find middle ground, our arguments continued. My husband was panicked at the idea of me pulling back and not having sex at all. The more the issue of sex became the battleground, the more I realised sex was all we had as the basis of our relationship. There was nothing else to sustain us.

Because of what I'd learnt, I could see many of the dysfunctional ways in which I and my family operated. Before the seminar I knew things were not okay, but after it I understood more of why things were not okay. I felt compassion for my children and tried not to react in the ways I used to when I couldn't cope. Instead of becoming numb and distant, or yelling and being rough to gain control, I responded more with patience and understanding about what was happening for them. I was becoming softer and more of a witness, rather than an unconscious participant.

I tried to break the negative patterns I had with my children by taking them for walks in the park or the bush. It also helped a lot when ugly arguments erupted between my husband and me. They were becoming more frequent and explosive as I resisted buying back into our old ways of relating.

Regardless of my husband's faults, I knew he was doing the best he knew how to do. His behaviour was an expression of his own wounding, insecurities and need to be loved, just as mine was. But it didn't change the fact that I was still not free from the anguish I carried, even though I'd had what was to me, a miraculous experience.

I felt suffocated by the intensity of my husband's needs and emotions. We didn't know how to reach each other or calm each other's fears. I agonised over thoughts of wanting to leave my marriage again.

The moral issue of marriage according to the religious view I'd been taught, had a strong hold on me. So did my fear of not being able to make it in the world on my own. Inside I was still a broken child. If I left, I would also be taking my husband's children away and it would be the second time he'd have to go through a divorce. Yet if I stayed, I felt I would die.

Whatever I chose had to be 'the right thing' for my children, my husband and me. Whichever choice I made, someone was going to lose. It was impossible to find a solution that made everything okay for everyone and it drove me to the depths of despair. How do I fix all the wrongs? How do I change the way I feel to make another happy, to please God, to heal my children? I wasn't even sure if leaving was what I really wanted. I needed time for the falling pieces of me to land so I could see who I was now and how I truly felt, but my husband's behaviour and need for sex was pushing me further out the door.

I was haunted by the antics my husband had used to manipulate me back when I'd left our marriage before. I didn't want any more dramas to be played out in front of our children, and I didn't want to continually feel like I was being held against my will. If I was going to stay, it had to be because it was where I wanted to be, for the right reasons and with my heart in it. I constantly prayed for guidance, asking God to tell me what to do. If He told me to stay, I'd stay. I would know it was the 'right' thing. If He told me I could go, I'd go and be free of guilt. Without His direction and approval, I was paralysed.

One night, the sound of talking voices wrestled me out of sleep, but not to the point of being fully awake. It was a rapid flow of constant dialogue that felt as though I was being given instruction. I couldn't make out what was being said, the words were coming too fast, and they seemed to be going to a different part of me.

I was aware of where I was, could feel my husband beside me and hear him breathe. I knew I wasn't dreaming, yet no matter how hard I tried to catch what was being said, I couldn't make it out. I struggled to wake fully but was unable. The clamour went on for some minutes until suddenly, the dialogue slowed.

A single female voice emerged from the chatter, saying the only thing God wanted from me, was for me to grow. The feeling I got was that flowering to my full potential, experiencing wonder, joy and happiness, was not only important but beloved. Being miserable, stunted and joyless was being dead and counterproductive to God/Life's purpose. It was also clear I had unencumbered freedom in making my choice. There was no hint of which action I should take. No expectation, judgment or condemnation, just support for whatever I chose, simply because I was free to choose.

I realised I was not going to be told what to do. I had to decide for myself, but still I couldn't act. I tried to meditate hoping to hear the same guiding voice from the workshop give me some kind of indication of what was right. I received nothing and felt more and more alone and torn inside.

One night, I listened to a meditation tape, again wanting to hear that same voice. When the tape finished I still had nothing. As I lay on my bed feeling completely deserted, I heard just two words, "Trust yourself". I flew off the bed in a rage and screamed, "Is that it? What the hell am I supposed to do with that?" It was the one thing I was most unable to do.

I extended my pursuit for direction by visiting a spiritual healer. She felt guided to tell me to go home and read Psalm 23. I went straight to the Bible still in my bookcase, a remnant from my days of trying to fit into a Christian Fellowship congregation. I found the Psalm and realised I knew it, I'd read it before. But this time it was stunning to me, and it made perfect sense;

The Lord is my shepherd; I shall not want.
He makes me to lie down in green pastures:
He leads me beside the still waters.
He restores my soul: He leads me in the paths
Of righteousness for his name's sake.
Yea, though I walk through the valley of
the shadow of death, I will fear no evil,
for you are with me.

It was the vision I'd had during my meditation at the Family of Origin Seminar. As I read the words, I could see myself again, peacefully at rest beside the still waters.

I used to think that anything from the Bible was suspect. Now I know there are inspired truths and spiritual lessons woven among the historical stories of its pages. They come from the hearts and minds of ordinary people who heard and felt what calls to them from the depths of their souls as they grappled with their own life's journey. Sadly, fear based religious groups with their penchant for control, who teach their way is the only way to know God, clutch onto their bibles and scriptures so tightly they squeeze the very life out of them.

I went back to the Spiritual healer, even though she was extremely confronting to my baggage about religion and the devil. Her home had odd paraphernalia and paintings that certainly would never be found in any church. Rather than do healing on me, she suggested we do some voice dialogue work, explaining this was a process that allowed us to discover the many aspects of our personality, especially the harmful and negative parts operating in the shadows. These were the parts that controlled and sabotaged our lives if we remained unconscious to them. I agreed, and so we began.

I was told to leave my chair and as I did, leave myself as Lyn, behind. I was to choose a different place in the room to sit, while remaining aware that Lyn was still in the other chair. As I sat down in my new chair, something strange happened. I felt completely different, huge, powerful and watchful. The healer began by saying hello and asking permission to speak with this new me, and as the conversation unfolded, I discovered a part in myself that was by far the largest part of who I was. The healer called it my killer critic.

The contempt the killer critic had for Lyn was obvious. It said Lyn had to be protected at all costs, especially from herself. She was completely incapable and without the killer critic, she would be nothing but jelly in her own skin, a bag of liquid on the floor. She literally had no bones and couldn't survive on her own.

The experience was a powerful insight into my self-loathing, and the defensive, mistrusting and angry way of being I'd developed. It was designed to shield something inside me that was small and fragile, something that had to be ferociously guarded because it couldn't defend itself.

The experience troubled me so much I never went back. I'd glimpsed into what seemed to be an incalculable pit, and I had no way of knowing how deep it went or what else it might contain. What if I fell in and couldn't find my way back out? I'd be lost in the darkness forever. It was all too sinister. The devil had to be lurking somewhere close by.

My decision to finally leave my marriage again was because I could no longer face what was happening in the home. I had waited for as long as I could for some indication from my husband that he was willing to back off. Instead, he continued to use guilt, tantrums, threats and the children, in his effort to gain back his power over me. I wanted a friend as a partner, not a man who was afraid of change and who only ever saw me sexually. I craved truly being seen, me the person, the soul of the woman I was yearning to become.

I needed to get out so I could breathe and be free of the guilt and shame of everyone's pain, especially my own, and the damage we were still causing our children. I thought if I left, the pain and chaos would end for everyone. I decided to start looking for a house to rent and began the search with our local paper. Mentally I was still sifting through all the things that had happened, the seminar, my spiritual experiences, fears of the devil, the past, dreams and nightmares.

Around the same time, I was reading a book called, *A Child of Eternity*, by Adriana Rocha and Kristi Jorde. It was the story of a young girl with autism, the details of her life and the extraordinary world she lived in within her mind. She had access to spiritual wisdom and knowledge that had no logical explanation. It furthered my hunger to know more about the spiritual world and as I read, I marvelled that I'd never known anything but fear.

While busy doing chores around the house I would puzzle over things I didn't understand and experience sudden flashes of comprehension. I began to appreciate something of spiritual energetics and the unseen forces that move within and around us. The insights helped me realise what not only my thoughts, but also my heart had been involved in creating and perpetuating within my environment, as well as myself.

Excited, I'd stop whatever I was doing and stand in awe, enjoying the feeling of revelation whilst at the same time, the light in the room would flicker or a toy in my sons' toy box would mysteriously activate. I knew Spirit was in my house. Whatever it was I had connected to in the workshop was still with me, coaxing me forward.

My ongoing spiritual education was confronting. The things I was learning were showing me how I had acted as a conduit for negative energy. It was startling. I began to feel a little less out of control, a little less hunted, and my depression had seemed to ease. Nevertheless, the problems in my marriage persisted.

Feeling stronger, I secretly arranged to look at a house for rent. Rather than take my now three-year-old twins with me, I organised to put them into day care for the afternoon. I rationalised it would be easier to manage on my own, besides which I felt guilty about what I was doing.

Reversing out of the driveway to go to the day care, I turned my head to look over my shoulder, and as I backed out, made eye contact with the twin who'd battled to survive after his birth. Shocked by the emptiness I saw, the intensity of sorrow so familiar to me, I slammed on the brakes.

Gently I asked what was wrong.

Without flinching he replied, "I died". His words stunned me.

"What?"

Again, it was the same.

"I died!"

I felt my heart pound and the hairs on the back of my neck raise. He said in a toneless voice,

"I want to go home."

Something was very wrong. I pointed to the house in front of us,

"We are home, see, there it is, right there."

His response sent chills down my spine.

"No. Back to the light."

Suddenly I realised the extent of how my small son was feeling. He was tired. Right from the start his existence in this world had been painful and precarious, with one event after another threatening to end his life. Looking at him, it seemed that way again now.

I had an abrupt realisation he didn't want to be here, he was just too desolate and sad. Gripped with terror, I had the worrying thought he was going to make himself sick so he could leave, and it filled me with panic.

"Please," I begged. "Stay with me, I need you."

In response my son nodded a very tiny nod, indicating he would. Relieved and feeling as if I had bought myself time, I drove on to the day care centre, arriving just as the children were being served lunch. I got the boys seated and waited until their meals were placed on the table in front of them, but I couldn't leave. My sons looked so dejected and lost. I knelt on the floor between them, wanting to stay until I felt it was okay to go.

It was my little boy who I'd had the conversation with in the car I was most concerned about. Watching him, I noticed he was following something with his eyes that seemed to be moving over the ceiling. He was transfixed by whatever it was only he could see.

I asked if it was beautiful. His response was a quiet and distant, but relieving, yes. I prayed that whatever it was around him was a reassuring presence, since I was unable to make him feel safe. He was vulnerable and sensitive. I had yet to learn how connected, energetically and spiritually, a mother is to her child, how that connection works, and what its purpose is. My other little boy was also affected, but in a different way. Outwardly, he seemed the stronger of the two, and not showing signs of a broken heart.

The house I went to see was perfect. It had a fenced yard for the boys and heating for the winter. I left my marriage for the third time, imagining I'd be better able to cope without the disturbing combat between my husband and myself.

That might have been true had I the guidance and support of someone, or some group, that knew and understood what I was going through, and what I still had to face. With only a tenuous link to the new things I'd discovered, I didn't know how, nor was I strong enough, to build on my fragile foundations alone.

I was still on medication, and toying with the idea that now might be a good time to stop taking it. I'd come to understand my problems were a direct result of my childhood, not because I was born deficient. Taking the tablets only reinforced my feelings of brokenness. I so much wanted to be normal, well, and manage on my own. But when it came down to it, I was more scared of not taking them, than I was of taking them.

One day, deeply involved with my troubled thoughts, I went to the bank to deposit a cheque. I was standing at the counter filling out my deposit slip, when I heard distressed mumblings to my left. I vaguely glanced towards the sounds and saw a frail old man fretting over filling out his own slip.

I turned my attention back to what I was doing, and within seconds, a male voice spoke in my mind and said, "Ask him if he wants any help." Startled, I looked over to the old man, and really saw him for the first time. He had quite a few cheques' needing to be deposited and it was just too much for him. His hands were shaking, and he looked anguished. Gently I asked if there was anything I could do. The man let out a great sigh of relief, and gratefully pushed his banking my way. I filled out his slip and as I talked with him, his distress disappeared.

When I left the bank, I was walking on air. I felt a deep sense of satisfaction and knew what Spirit was trying to show me. When we are lost in consuming self-involvement, we are blind to the needs and plight of those around us, while in helping others, we ultimately help ourselves. It is the remedy for soul destroying self-pity, and a path that leads us out of the pit of isolation and despair.

I tried to remain upbeat and positive and stay aware of Spirit in my life. I thought a lot about the things I'd experienced and what it all ultimately meant, but I could feel myself slipping as each day went by.

Our lives collapsed into chaos instead of becoming the welcome sanctuary I'd hoped for. Once the journey from the shadow lands begins, life can become unexpectedly rough, taking twists and turns previously unimagined. I was inexperienced enough to think that the initial contact with my inner child meant my journey was nearly over, but it had only just begun.

I found myself alone with emotionally insecure and destructive little boys, and an anxious young daughter desperately needing love and attention. My sons' on-the-go behaviour frequently resulted in the house being torn apart. They took great delight in stripping their beds of sheets and blankets, and the walls in their bedroom were gouged with holes where the plaster had been broken by the impact of flying toys. They ransacked the chook pen I'd restored to house chickens, and smashed their eggs whenever they could.

Guilt and inadequacy pounded me into the ground until I, too, was out of control. I was angry I was alive, angry I'd had spiritual experiences that left me hanging, angry because of my stolen childhood, and angry with my children for being my responsibility when all I wanted to do was disappear.

Alone with my confusion, I fell into a hole of crushing penitence for being such an incapable person, for being so useless and broken. I pushed the twins in front of the video player to keep them occupied. It seemed the only way to keep them out of trouble. Unable to mother them I buried myself in more books, desperately seeking something. In my inability to cope, wrath became my way of reacting to the feelings and problems I was unable to deal with. My daughter and I grew further apart as I relentlessly raged and expected far too much from her.

I had moments when I thought I knew what I was supposed to do. I had to live simply and within my means, spending time in meditation and prayer to develop my trust in, and connection to God. It was up to me to strengthen that relationship and make the decision to stop fighting within myself, but it was something I just couldn't do.

I became more and more separated from my feelings of connection to Spirit. Engrossed in my struggles, I was resentful all the time and had no patience with anything. I was suffering from a major depressive illness and fighting ghosts I couldn't see.

I asked myself the same questions repeatedly. Was it against God to leave my marriage? Was it a sin? Would I go to hell? Was I the one to blame for everything? What about the damage I'd done to my children by taking them away from their home, breaking up the family again and again. I could not live with the churning thoughts rampaging in my mind.

Each passing second was spent in fear, trying to hold everything together, trying to control everyone's behaviour, including my own. The more I tried to control the worse things got. I wanted to stay in a tight ball, but it was impossible with children. Their behaviour demanded I stay present. They needed me and were relentless in trying to pull me out of myself, and I resented having to come out. Being in the world was too painful for me, so deep were my feelings of failure about being a worthwhile human being.

During the Family of Origin work, I'd discovered grief, degrees of forgiveness, loss and sadness, but I had not yet consciously confronted or experienced my buried rage. Once real healing begins, all levels of the healing process must be worked through.

Blind fury surfaced, and it was coming out in the most destructive ways, constantly feeding itself. It kept me lost in a spiralling cycle of shame. I had no one to steer me through it, or to help me understand.

I had already been a passive-aggressive person. It was an aspect of my behaviour that came out in response to the stresses of my marriage. After the birth of my first child, along with undiagnosed Postnatal Depression; fear, intolerance and impatience in mothering also appeared. What I was experiencing now was volcanic and unrestrained.

Battered by a constant barrage of mishap after mishap, without ever having enough time to fully recover from one event before the next one hit, I was living as the effect of accumulative causes. An angry woman embittered by constant troubling thoughts and an unrelenting voice in my head that cited every conceivable shortcoming I could possibly have. My culpability for every wrong was lethal.

I had to do something. We couldn't go on the way we were much longer.

One dull morning, I was sitting in my car in front of our deli pondering the mess of my life, when I picked up the local paper off the car seat beside me. I began flipping through its pages. In the health section, I found an advertisement for counselling that began with the heading; *Are You Tired of Fighting All the Voices in Your Head?* It had my immediate attention.

I took the paper home and rang the number listed. A woman's voice answered and an hour later, I'd told her the basics of my story. She talked to me about Inner Child work, and considering my vision, I took it as a sign.

I began counselling with her the following week, with two-hour in-depth sessions. I was still carrying a great deal of fear and uncertainty, not sure if I was safe yet from the clutches of the devil.

Chapter 9

DESCENT TO HELL

Suzie was unusual to say the least, nothing like any kind of therapist I'd ever seen. Everything about her was earthy and alternative, her bare feet, unshaven legs, soft silky mauve and lavender-hued clothing, and her long salt and pepper-coloured hair that flowed in one length down the middle of her back. Her tall stature oozed power and authority and her appearance agitated my fears about anything that was different.

When our eyes first met, a strong feeling of unease bore through me. The impact almost threw me back. Her dark brown eyes seemed impenetrable, guarded somehow, but I pushed the discomfort aside and told myself not to be so paranoid.

In my first session I spoke about my personal situation, the Family of Origin Intensive I'd attended and the vision of my inner child. I expressed my longing to heal my life and find a way to bring that part of myself back. I wanted to stay clear on the instruction I'd been given by the voice at the Intensive, but Suzie had her own ideas.

In her view, it was better for me to go back to the past and work on recovering any forgotten memories still buried in my subconscious. Without uncovering them, they'd continue to poison and run my life. I handed myself over as I have always done. We began with visualisation techniques.

When I closed my eyes and followed her guidance, I immediately saw a little girl hidden in an old well, huddled in darkness with her back resting against damp, stony walls. She was the same child I'd seen in my vision at the Family of Origin seminar. But in this image her arms were wrapped tightly around drawn-up knees, her face lowered and hidden between them. Everything about her was dirty - her skin, her matted and tangled hair and her grubby, ragged clothes. This child was hidden in heartbreak, her sense of aloneness profound.

It soon became apparent the little girl in the well was not going to respond to any effort made by Suzie to rescue her. She was unaware of anything outside her own existence, totally lost in the emptiness of her despair. The image made me remember an exercise I'd been a part of in group therapy years before at the Sexual Assault Referral Centre.

At the time, we'd been asked to draw a pot or vase that reflected our inner child. I had instinctively drawn a well in the ground with a lid on it that was completely sealed. I couldn't understand why I'd drawn it, and had no idea there was a child inside.

Suzie moved me on to non-dominant handwriting during our second session, to try and talk with the part of me hidden in the well. This form of writing is where the adult writes a question using the dominant hand, and the part of us we are trying to access, or that is ready to come forward, answers the question using the other hand. The process allows us to delve into parts of ourselves that are submerged and out of our awareness.

The intention was to create a dialogue between the little girl in the well and myself as the adult. Suzie said we had to foster a sense of trust between the separated parts, so we could bring the child part up into safety. But all did not go to plan.

What came through instead, was completely unexpected. The words I wrote with my non-dominant hand were poetic and almost biblical in language. When asked, it identified itself as my Light, and urged me to release the chains around my heart.

What I was writing astounded me, but I was scared about where it came from. It could be a bad part in me playing tricks, or worse, it could be the devil himself, trying to lure me to him. Even though I was sceptical, I wanted to explore it. It felt non-judging and supportive;

speaking in concepts I seemed to understand with a quiet strength and wisdom beyond the ordinary. It even offered me love. Suzie wanted to steer away from it.

Each time Suzie tried to get more deeply into my subconscious I felt rushed, manipulated and unsafe, so the wise part would become present. When she later used voice dialogue techniques to try to talk with the wounded parts of me, this same wise and ever-present guardian would speak instead.

I was stunned at the feeling of tranquillity and other worldliness of that part of me. I felt safe and protected. Suzie got increasingly frustrated and annoyed, telling me I was blocking her attempts to help me. I had to drop my guard and trust her.

I began to feel more uneasy and tried to get Suzie to take me where I wanted to go, but her strength was far more powerful than the little amount of self-belief I had. She was the counsellor and the authority. According to her, the methods she used were the only way to heal. She'd studied and researched all others and found them lacking. I had to do the work her way if I was ever going to get better, so, in believing I didn't know what was right for me; I continued to follow her lead.

In a following session, Suzie mentioned something completely unexpected. We were using visualisation processes with the little girl in the well and at a particularly vulnerable moment, she mentioned my father. She had already made up her mind he was the key and she wanted to cut straight to the core of the problem.

Her eyes shone darker than usual and they were intently focused on me. Shocked, I immediately pulled out of the process and felt my feelings of mistrust rise. I knew my father had done some awful things but what she was inferring wasn't among them. I felt an inkling of Suzie's purpose. If I'd reacted in the way she'd hoped, she would have had total control.

Some days later, a peculiar thing happened. I was woken from sleep by a loud and insistent male voice yelling, "Volunteer! Volunteer!"

The word kept repeating, over and over, until I responded, asking "Volunteer? You want me to volunteer? Volunteer where?" The reply was very clear, "Hills Community Support Group."

In a half-wakeful state I thought to myself, why would I want to volunteer there? It's a place for geriatrics! I was mortified, but realised it was a message I should not ignore. Feeling ashamed of my reaction, I got out of bed with a resolve to follow the instruction.

Later that day I picked up the phone, wishing I didn't have to. I didn't feel like helping anybody, I couldn't even help myself. It felt like an imposition to be told this was what I had to do, but I dialled the number and spoke to the woman who coordinated the volunteer program. We made a time to meet the following day.

As it turned out, the Hills Community Support Group was desperate to have someone on a Monday when the frail-aged came for social interaction, many of whom suffered from dementia and other mental health problems.

It dawned on me during the interview that Mondays were my counselling session days with Suzie. I couldn't see it being a problem so assured the coordinator it would be fine, I'd change things around to be available. I left the meeting feeling surprisingly light and looking forward to starting.

I never made it back. I rang Suzie and told her about being woken with the instruction to do this particular volunteer work, and asked if I could change my day with her so I could keep the commitment. Her reaction was a surprise. Without even considering it, she said no, all her other days were booked. Monday was the only day available to me. If I wanted to heal I had to stick to my work with her. With regret and a bad feeling in my heart, I rang the volunteer coordinator to tell her I couldn't get Mondays free after all.

My sessions continued with Suzie, as did her efforts to open me up to the darkest parts of my wounding as quickly as possible. Through the weeks that followed, I slid further into her world, but the wise part kept me safe from being made totally vulnerable to her matriarchal control.

Even as I was going through the processes with her, I was aware of this part in me watching, assessing and filing away intuitive understandings about Suzie's agenda. It was acting as an independent observer, gathering information, understanding and awareness, yet I was unable to act on the knowledge. I hadn't grown enough to be able to bridge the gap between my wounded child self, and my innate, discerning, wise self.

As the sessions continued, I struggled to remember what I'd learnt at the Family of Origin seminar, and battled to keep in mind what it was I was originally looking for.

I continued to read more books, mostly purchased from New Age book shops, which added to my confused state of mind. But one day, while walking past a regular book store in a shopping centre, I noticed a sale sign in large red letters hanging above a stall littered with paperbacks. Curious, I walked over and started to browse. The first one I picked up was titled, *I've Found the Keys, Now Where's the Car?* The subheading read, *10 Keys to Personal Fulfilment, Happiness and Success; How to unlock your potential and turn change into opportunity*. The book was written by Vicki Bennett and only five dollars, too good a bargain to pass up.

I lay in bed that night with my usual muddled thoughts and images dancing in my mind. The book was on the dressing table on the other side of the room. I looked over to it and argued with myself about whether I should read it.

I got up, disorientated and cloudy, took the book and got back under the covers. As I flipped through the pages, I felt a small spark of interest, but it died quickly. There was nothing to take me in, to lull me with dreamy, other worldly ideas. In fact, it was quite the opposite. It was practical, down to earth and instructive.

Closing the book I began to argue with myself again, when out of the corner of my eye I saw the outline of a very tall, white figure, standing right next to where my head lay on the pillow. It moved down to the end of my bed, rounded the corner and moved along the bed end, disappearing just as suddenly as it had appeared. As I'd watched it move I got the clear impression it was urging me to read. Even though it was only an apparition that had no facial features or distinctions, I knew it had looked right at me in earnest. Startled, I re-opened the book.

Over the next few days, I managed to read a little more than half the book before losing interest again. I put it away and continued to stay stuck in my cycle of looking for something, and not finding it.

I didn't know it at the time, but I wanted to be lost. I didn't want to find my way to the surface. I didn't want to live in the real world. Everything in the book had been about living, how to take charge of your life, take responsibility and be proactive. The truth was I was more afraid of living than I was of dying. With the closing of the book I said no to life and continued to drown, while Suzie continued to delve into my subconscious.

I became more unstable, more afraid and unable to cope with my children. I told Suzie my concerns, explained how it felt to be inside me, lost from everything, but she told me not to worry. If she felt I wasn't coping she would ring the women from the fortnightly women's group I was also now attending with her, and have them contact me as a support network. But it never happened.

I was spending substantial amounts of time incapacitated, curled up on my bed in the foetal position, moaning like an injured animal. The emotional pain I felt was excruciating, as if something had its claws in my chest, tearing me open from the inside.

The murky waters of my past had been stirred so much I couldn't close my eyes without seeing the evil, ugly, twisted faces of witches and devils in the swirling mists of black. It was like living through my childhood again, only the surroundings were different, and my body grown. The taste of fear was the same, the terror was the same, and the feeling of being in danger was the same. I felt like I was wading through dark tunnels full of sewage and as I waded, I was becoming more and more lost in the bowels of the underground. I was travelling further and further away from the light.

I put my twins into full-time day care, incapable of caring for them myself. I lost control over every aspect of my life. Thoughts ran wild as

I contemplated all manner of things to do with my past, spiritual issues, the contents of the books I'd read and the darkness that plagued my mind.

Many a night was spent in fear and prayer, trying desperately to connect to something I could hold on to. Sometimes I sat at a desk in my bedroom, poring over journal writings and Rune stone readings, crying with my face buried in my hands. I sank further and further, feeling the darkness deepen as it passed over me and entered unopposed into my body. Something was terribly wrong.

My feelings of guilt and badness increased because I'd put my boys in day care, and I continued to scream at my daughter, incapable of loving her. I felt split in two with one side of me criticising the other, a constant barrage of inner talk that was at war. On one side, I knew I was doing wrong, but it was the lesser side, I had no power over my volatile wounded rage. It had become the larger part of who I was.

The deeper I disappeared, the more I felt invaded by the darkness. I had no defences against it. I tried to pull away from my involvement with Suzie several times, but she would coaxingly offer counselling sessions over the phone, eventually talking me back. I would be left feeling frustrated and manipulated, but I didn't know how to be well on my own. I needed something, someone to hold on to. I could not be alone.

Our sessions began to include more about my broken marriage and the heavy guilt I felt. Suzie introduced me to another model she used in her counselling approach. It seemed that to fully heal myself and my life, I would be better to go back to my marriage and work it out using Imago therapy techniques.

Imago therapy is based on the principle that we unconsciously choose partners who are a compilation of our primary caretakers in emotionally significant ways. Each one of us carries this subconscious image, looking for a match. When we come across it, we experience attraction and fall in love. It's when the idyllic love phase wears off that we discover our love partner is the one person in the world who can drive us nuts the most. They, more than anyone, push the buttons of our deepest hurts, fears and insecurities. The process of Imago Relationship Therapy uses this understanding to heal each partner's psychological and spiritual wounding, thereby transforming the relationship.

Suzie stressed if I didn't heal my wounds with my current partner, I was doomed to continue to repeat the same issues with the next man to enter my life. Afraid and confused, I went back to my husband.

It wasn't long before my husband and I were in couples counselling with Suzie. I was filled with hope and wanted my marriage to work, but as time went on, I couldn't shake the feeling that something was not quite right. My husband was constantly writing cheques to pay for all the work we were doing with her. It became too much of a financial strain, so he began to exchange his time and building skills for the sessions we were having.

The life we led with Suzie became more extensive. There were gatherings at her house where we socialised with other people who attended regular counselling, weekend workshops and group sessions with Suzie, and my husband began to attend a group for men led by Suzie's partner.

In my fortnightly women's group, I saw adults regressed to traumatised children in a matter of seconds, playing out their childhood wounding with each other again and again. Suzie used Voice dialogue techniques to achieve this. Having worked with them over time, she knew which buttons to push to get an instant response.

There were times when the level of worship and dependency the women had for Suzie, shone in her eyes as supremacy. I knew the awe they felt for her was misplaced, and that because they were reduced to a child state in her presence, she represented a god-like parent figure. To a wounded child still active in an adult body, somebody like Suzie was safety and security.

In our group work, Suzie always sat at a higher level than anyone else, like a Queen on her throne with her subjects about her feet, and always with her back to the door, facing the women. She covered the exit and held sway over the room, subtle techniques that created the energy dynamics to control and manipulate. She was in charge. It was her group and we were her women.

We had our egos massaged on a regular basis by being told how special we were. We were doing the real growth work while everyone else out there in the world was only plodding along. We were at a much higher stage of spiritual development than most, and amazing because we were progressing so fast. Our group was pretty much the cream.

Most of the women were seeing Suzie on a one-to-one basis and had been for some time. It seemed to me the need to play out childhood scenarios repeatedly in such a powerful way was hypnotic, addictive and destructive. The whole set-up was almost a lifestyle, something you never grew beyond.

While I still resisted giving over my full power to Suzie, I was a keen observer in what took place with everyone else, yet I became more and more troubled and angry inside my own childhood wounding. Suzie was the mother, I was the child, and while I was not giving myself permission to get fully into process work, I was aware of a growing agitation and resentment toward her.

Rather than tell Suzie how I felt, I internalised it. I was angry because I was in so much pain, and as the mother, she didn't see it. She did not protect me or comfort me. She was distant and calculating, her hugs cold and empty. Everything about her was shallow and self-serving. The child in me hated her for not coming to its aid, for not being what she said she was, for not following through on the things she said she would. I was still invisible.

The pressure was building. The night of the next women's group I got in my car and drove aimlessly around the dark streets feeling disturbed, not knowing how to deal with myself or how to stop what I was feeling. I didn't want to go to the group. I didn't want to go home. I just wanted to evaporate. I was on a merry-go-round I couldn't get off. Reluctantly, not having anywhere else to go, I turned the car in the direction of Suzie's house.

Work had already begun with some of the women when I walked into the room. I looked around and felt jealousy. They were her prize students because they were always prepared to go into childhood and work their histories. Suzie clearly favoured them.

As soon as I sat down, I connected with my seething anger and aimed it at Suzie like a dagger. At some point I must have been given an opportunity to speak. All the accumulated emotion erupted. I started to tell Suzie off because to me she was the source of my pain. I was angry at being manipulated and filled with rage over her attempts to control and twist my reality into her truth. I was just as angry with myself for letting her.

As the rage unleashed my self-hatred came to the surface and I began to savagely pound my chest with my fists, but it was really her I wanted to destroy. I learnt in childhood I couldn't win with a parent, so I had only myself to hate. Eventually, Suzie instructed some of the women to hold my hands. She was afraid of me and never moved from her chair.

In my mind, the devil I feared began talking to me and laughing at them. They were all so stupid. Suzie told me I had an opportunity to process how I was feeling, that it was my choice to heal and do something differently. I had everyone's attention now and their support. It was my time. They lay me down on the floor in the middle of the room and sat around me in a circle.

I was asked to close my eyes and describe what I saw inside myself. All I could see was the familiar blackness, deep, thick and murky. There was no light, not anywhere in my body. I felt poison in my hatred, in my rage.

Each woman began to talk in turn, one following on from the other saying in the form of prayer and invocation that the darkness was to leave and be replaced by light. Someone mentioned God, and in my mind I laughed harder. What did they know of God?

Nothing they said worked. The darkness wouldn't budge and what I thought was the devil in me continued to laugh, yet I was present, and the wise part witnessed all that was taking place. Someone suggested using a spiritual vacuum cleaner to suck out the dark, so they used visualisation to do just that. While they were busy cleaning me out the devil continued to laugh in my head.

Suzie asked me where the darkness was coming from, and I had an instant realisation it wasn't mine. It was my father's. The understanding came powerfully to me as his presence suddenly broke through. I received a deep sense of his conflicted and wounded rage, the torment of his buried childhood experiences, and the religion he'd grown up with.

My father had fought a battle with dark devils that got the better of him, driving him to alcoholism and violence. At the Family of Origin workshop, I'd learnt my parents carried wounds, but in this moment, I really experienced the truth of it. I saw that unresolved wounding carries from one generation to the other energetically. It was passed on to my father, and through him, it was passed on to me. I also received a sense of how this process occurs, but what I didn't understand, was what the catalyst was that caused my father's demons to become so completely mine.

I began to cry, feeling only compassion and sorrow for the both of us, and through my tears, I silently spoke to his wounded inner child, as if the words in my mind could somehow reach back through time. And I spoke to his soul in the present. I told him I forgave him, that I loved him, and understood his pain.

I heard someone's voice from among the women ask if I was able to see some light inside. By this time I was much calmer, not because of the process they'd put me through, but because I'd had insight into what was happening within myself. It never made it go away, but it gave me understanding and relief.

I told the women I was fine, that I'd felt the darkness become light. I didn't want to disappoint them. But neither could I explain what I'd just experienced. Whenever I had those sorts of insights and understandings, Suzie would knock them down. She was threatened by my ability to interpret my own experience.

It is empowering to know you can interpret your own experience, and it's a huge gift and act of love when a counsellor or therapist gives a client permission to trust their own knowing. It was something Suzie was not able to do. She needed to be the only one who had any power or knowledge.

At one point my daughter was also dragged into the therapy process. We began working with Suzie in sessions of our own to try to heal our damaged mother-daughter relationship. She hated it, but I told her it was for our good. I desperately wanted to fix what I thought I'd broken. We only went together a handful of times, giving up in the end because of the cost and my daughter's discomfort and dislike of being in counselling.

I felt relieved for her to be out of it. This was my nightmare not hers. It had become clear to me it was more harmful than helpful for her to be taken down this road against her will. I continued to plod along alone, protecting myself, not quite giving myself over to Suzie. She and I were locked in a power struggle and we both knew it.

It was also apparent that going back to my marriage and the family home had been a mistake. Our situation had degenerated into an even worse state than before I'd left.

I spent substantial portions of time out of my body or submerged in my books. My interest had switched from spiritual ponderings to human development. I was now reading self-help material. I read books written by M. Scott Peck M.D., John Bradshaw, Harville Hendrix PhD, Harriet Lerner, and Hal and Sidra Stone PhD.

I learned more about addictions, abuse and family systems, but most of all I learnt through reading and processing, how to recognise myself. It was like holding up a mirror. The reflection was such that it was as unbearable to see the loss of me, as much as it was to see the things I'd become.

Much of what I learned I saw in the dynamics between my husband and myself, the role I played in the triangle between my daughter, her father and I, the enmeshment and lack of boundaries. I recognised my childhood wounding and the ways in which it coloured my objectivity and parenting. But it seemed the more I read, the more puzzled and overwhelmed I became with the complexities of human emotional and psychological development.

Overloaded with the burden I was carrying my body simply began to drop to the floor. My depression had become intolerably severe and I had little energy left to function.

Many people do not understand the force that powers the body. If you were a medical person, you would cite the major organs and circulatory systems as being responsible for maintaining human life and of course, they do, but only in part. The human body also has an electrical system without which, the physical processes would cease. This same energy system is plugged into a much larger source of power. It is the same with our cars. We keep them fuelled, service them, tune them, change the spark plugs and oil, but if the car's connection to its power source, the battery, is impeded, the car no longer starts. For all intents and purposes, it is dead, yet its machinery is in perfect working order. The same is true for our bodies.

My battery was almost dry, the source of my power, negligible. I grieved my dying because I wanted to live, I just didn't know how. I had no idea a human being could get into the condition I was in. I was buried alive and no one could see or hear me.

It was at this time I dreamt I was in a different country with my children and my husband. We were the only ones who spoke English. Everyone else spoke a foreign language. I was standing well apart from my family and our tour guide and interpreter, who happened to be Suzie, and was watching them as they discussed the views.

Suddenly I heard one of my sons scream. I recognised with terror the pain in the sound and went running to him. It was not the sound of physical pain, but agonising, spiritual pain. My husband became annoyed and told me not to over-react; the boy had simply banged his head.

Pulling my son close, I ran my hand over the top of his head, feeling for a bump. Instead, my hand disappeared into a deep gash in his skull. He was in serious trouble and I knew it. No one would listen to me, they couldn't see the wound. I begged for someone to tell me where the nearest hospital was, but no one understood what I was saying. Picking my son up, I began to run, and as I ran, he became smaller, no longer a little boy but an infant in my arms. He was dying, bleeding to death from the wound. I knew it was up to me to save him.

The dream was about me. The child in me was dying. The wound in the top of my son's head represented the life force leaving my own body.

No one in my life comprehended what was wrong with me, or what I was saying because we were speaking different languages. My wound was being treated with a complete lack of understanding. I got the dream's message loud and clear. It was up to me to save myself. I could not continue to put myself into the hands of other people, hoping they could heal me. The task was mine.

I talked to Suzie and my husband about the dream in our next session, giving my interpretation of what I believed it meant. Suzie swiftly informed me it meant something entirely different. It was pointless trying to speak. My insides were twisting and churning as still I continued to allow myself to be overpowered by someone else's agenda.

Soon after, I had another dream. I was on holiday on a tropical island, and while out and about I passed by a little shop with the most beautiful array of fabrics I'd ever seen. They were stacked invitingly on a stall by the door. The colours were bright and stunning, many with fine gold thread woven in intricately detailed designs, a feast for the eyes.

But there was one specific roll of fabric, almost obscured by the eye-catching colours of the rest, that caught my eye. Its colours were a combination of soft and soothing blues, giving off a feeling of pure and uncomplicated simplicity. Looking at it filled me with warmth and touched me on the inside with a quiet serenity. I knew it was special. I took the fabric into the shop and asked how much it cost.

To my dismay, I didn't have enough money, so requested it be kept for me while I went to get some more. When I returned, I asked for the fabric. Smiling, the woman reached up behind her where many more rolls of brightly coloured fabric sat on shelving across the back wall. Picking one up, she passed it to me, but I knew instantly it wasn't the right one.

It looked like the fabric I'd chosen, but it lacked that same indefinable presence, without which it was dead, just another piece of fabric. I told her I wanted the right one, the one I'd given her. The woman's smile disappeared. She began to argue with me, insisting it was the right one and urging me to buy it.

I looked up at all the rolls of fabric on the wall and saw mine had been concealed and lost among them. The message of my dream was undeniable. I had to trust myself and not allow myself to be tricked into buying what is presented to me just because it resembles the truth. I was to be very careful of appearances and stay true to the determination of wanting only what is real, not a replication. It was also obvious this would be the hard road, one where I would come up against opposition and the constant challenge to trust myself.

I became even more introspective and absorbed in my books. One book came to me as I browsed a bookstore looking for something new. It was titled, *People of the Lie*, written by one of my favourite authors, M. Scott Peck, M.D.

Thumbing through the book's pages, the word 'evil' repetitively hit my eyes. I was terrified of evil, and what was he doing writing about such things? Shuddering, I put the book back on the shelf, turned and walked away. Yet despite my fear, a strong urge to go back and pick it up wouldn't let me go. Flipping the book from one hand to the other, I asked Spirit if I had to read it. My body responded with the familiar sensation I often experienced when being led to a book I was supposed to read. I'd come to trust this process, so in trepidation, bought the book and took it home.

I began reading that night and disappeared, pulled down into a place where nothing existed except for the words on the pages. It was the most emotionally painful book I'd ever read but I couldn't understand why. When I finally finished it, my mind wouldn't shut off, even though I was fatigued and washed out by the experience. I had a nagging feeling I was missing something essential the book was trying to tell me, and I unmistakably felt a presence behind the attempt to convey its message.

Exhausted, I silently begged to be put to sleep and within seconds, I passed out.

I knew I was gone from my children and completely unavailable to their needs. While immersed in my book, a distant part of me saw and heard the chaos around me, had seen the way my husband struggled to cope or understand. But I was powerless to respond. We were in two different dimensions and nothing could pull me out of mine into theirs.

I dropped to the floor more often in overwhelming grief, not able to hold my body up on my own any longer. The huge effort to stay afloat and mentally comprehend what was happening to me was literally killing me, very slowly, very painfully, spiritually and psychologically.

Each morning I woke disappointed I was alive. I was so tired I desperately wanted to die, but I knew I would never, could never, intentionally take my own life. It was a deep knowing in my soul that it would be the ultimate act of selfishness and self-betrayal.

It seemed everyone wanted pieces of me, but there was no 'me' left. I had no energy, and no heart. Exhausted I couldn't read anymore, couldn't think anymore. I was mentally overloaded and close to the point of shutdown.

Some nights I left the house because the fighting and arguing was more than I could take. I didn't know how to make it stop, how to protect my children from their father or my own self-absorbed state of depression. We lived two kilometres out of town and I would drive the dark roads with my headlights off, wishing I had the courage to hit a tree.

I would turn up the radio and scream the most primal screams, giving voice to the sound that constantly lived unexpressed in my head, until my throat was hoarse and swollen and my voice a painful rasp. Strangely, my mouth would open wide until my jaw could stretch no further. It felt like something inside was trying to get out. I prayed a lot. I struggled with thoughts of the devil and dark imaginings while asking God to protect me. I was fighting for my life, my sanity, and my soul.

One night in a couple's session with my husband, I revealed to Suzie my secret crazy thoughts about being possessed, and my fear of the potential for evil inside me. I told her about my struggle to stay in control of my sanity. I was scared my husband might use it against me, but I was desperate. Suzie offered me an exorcism. I was relieved to finally have it out in the open and agreed to have it arranged.

The next day I had an unexpected telephone conversation with a woman I'd made friends with from the women's group. She'd only ever attended once, but we'd clicked and stayed in touch. Her reason for not coming back was her unease about the way Suzie operated. She did not feel safe with her.

I told her about my dark thoughts and fears of being possessed by the devil, and that I was going to have an exorcism arranged by Suzie. My friend was horrified and begged me to listen to some of her old writings from her journal, hoping it would help me understand.

As she read, I was speechless. It was as though she was talking about me. Her words described the same dark contamination, from the ends of her hair down to the very tips of her toes. Every cell in her body had been filled with evil. She was a vile creature, and because it was so dark, she too once believed she was possessed by the devil.

Through her current therapist, she came to understand it was not the devil or possession at all, but the very real energy she was perpetuating by the force of her mind, powered by her own self-hatred and virulent self-rejection. It was her way of punishing herself, blaming herself for the fact that her father had raped her as a little girl. Once she realised the truth, her fear of being possessed vanished and it freed her to do some real work around the fear, rage and grief she'd buried.

Incredulous, I recognised that it was I, with the power of my own mind, with the strength of my own self-hatred, ignorant beliefs and fears, who was killing me. I lay on the floor and laughed at the absurdity of agreeing to be exorcised, only to dissolve into tears of wretched grief. For the first time for as long as I could remember, I was free from the clutches of the devil.

With the understanding that all the sorrow I'd felt over the years was based on lies, that I'd actually believed myself to be unworthy of life, a new and more poignant grief crushed my heart. I cried for all the damage caused, for the girl child and for me now, knowing I'd spent a lifetime rejecting myself, hating myself so intensely that insanity or death was preferred over living. Mourning impacted full force.

Whatever energy I had left was lost in my deeper grief. It was agonising to comprehend just how much my childhood had taken from me, and the harm I'd caused because of it.

I still knew God was real, that the spiritual world existed, but I felt a profound sense of failure over my life. Somehow, I'd let God down. I didn't even have the strength anymore to wish I were dead. I totally gave up.

Soon after, I sensed something in the air. My husband and I had been fighting, pulling at each other emotionally, while in the background, our children had the run of the house. Finally, when everyone was in bed asleep, I sat with a book and tried to read, but I was unable to focus.

I wasn't breathing very well. Tiredness dragged on my body. I took myself off to my daughter's bathroom to shower, wanting to avoid being near my husband in case he woke. It was close to midnight.

In the shower, the hot water soothed my tired body and as the droplets of warmth hit my skin, I was grateful I could still feel that much. It was like being massaged and caressed at the same time. Not having enough strength left to stand, I dropped to the shower floor, curled into a tight foetal ball and fully let go.

I thought about how sorry I was for not being strong enough to go on. I apologised to God over and over, asking Him to forgive me for failing at whatever it was I was meant to do with my life. I said I was sorry for everything I'd done, for being a bad mother and a weak person. I told Him I couldn't do it anymore, I was too weary and couldn't carry the pain any longer. I just wanted it to be over.

During the many weeks leading up to this event, it seemed I had not only my own pain, but also that of the world. Everyone's suffering seemed to be mine, tearing me apart. I'd not been able to listen to the news or read a newspaper. Hearing of any incident where someone was hurt or killed, I would feel their suffering, feel the dying, and grief for those left behind. Even walking through a shopping center had become unbearable. I would feel the weight of everyone's burdens, and every time I heard a child cry, I would cry, too.

Now it was over. My body was covering the plughole and the bottom of the shower was steadily filling with water, rising to envelop my face, but I didn't care. I had no will left and no strength to endure any more suffering.

I knew when my body was discovered in the morning it would appear I'd drowned. But my spirit was already in the process of leaving. I was barely breathing at all and fully understood I had only to choose not to take the next breath to be free. I closed my eyes, and as I continued to ask for forgiveness, I drifted away.

The darkness was warm and welcoming, surrounding me, pulling me into its silent embrace. It was like floating down and disappearing into a large vat of warm treacle. I felt at peace to be there, receiving the emptiness of sweet death. My awareness had dulled, no longer able to feel the water hit my skin.

Drifting, I dimly recognised a faint, cold breeze brush my upturned cheek. It was in such contrast to the lack of feeling everywhere else on my body. Somewhere on the edge of my mind, I registered it happening, but not enough to pull me out. I didn't want it to. Instead, I descended further into the blissful warmth of the dark, travelling deeper into its welcome.

Again, I felt the cold breeze on my cheek, this time a little more insistently. I wasn't able to respond, but I was more conscious it was happening. I struggled. I didn't want to come back. I didn't want to be aware. There was only suffering in being alive.

The breeze began to blow sharper and more persistent, until I was provoked enough to again be aware of my body. I wondered how it was possible. The bathroom was small and the door was closed. The window was shut and the shower door pulled all the way across the cubicle. Steam filled the room and condensation dripped down the walls from the heat of the water. Where had the breeze come from, and how had it touched only that one small spot on my upturned cheek?

Suddenly I realised what was happening. In my mind I groaned and complained I just wanted to be allowed to go. I was warm and cosy in the darkness of nothing, but the breeze insistently continued to blow. The next thing I knew I was standing up and turning the shower taps off. I don't remember how I got up, but I remember thinking, "Okay! Okay! If I have to keep going, that is what I will do."

What happened to me was not a suicide attempt. I didn't go to the shower with the intention to die. It never crossed my mind. My spirit simply gave out from heartache and extreme exhaustion. Once down, I did not have the power to get up on my own. My soul cried out to God, and in that moment, I lay fully in His hands.

The only thing on my mind when I felt the presence of death, was immense sorrow. Not just for my own wrongs and weaknesses, but because in that moment I had come to a much fuller understanding of what it means to be human. We are all vulnerable, travelling a landscape inherent with risk, trials and pitfalls. To be here requires courage. There are no guarantees for any of us.

For the next two weeks I had moments where I was still closely connected to death. If it is called in, it has a habit of trying to lull you back with the promise of peace. I was still very weak and vulnerable. Sometimes I would give into my tiredness, the beckoning of death, and lay down on the couch in the lounge room. Thankfully I'd close my eyes, my breath would again almost cease, and I'd begin to drift to the dark place. I knew I could go if I wanted to.

But whenever I gave in to the exhaustion, a huge gold and white explosion, like a fireworks chrysanthemum, would flash to the side of my vision. There was no sound and its image was not present in my time and space, yet it appeared so I could see it. The flashes were reminders, telling me to get up and on my feet. Something was watching over me, pushing me to keep moving. The bright flashing light ceased, when I ceased to give in.

The depression and despair I suffered was beyond anything I could have conceived a human being experiencing. Parts of me were split off and lost, separated from each other. I was living out the isolation of the little girl buried in the underground well. Nothing existed, not God, not man, not the universe, only the torment of being buried alive and alone.

I had my spiritual essence, the child in white, in a hidden grove on the spiritual plane without the knowledge of how she came to be there, or how to get her back. The pain I felt was my soul screaming to be made whole again, to be reunited with the missing parts of itself.

Chapter 10

FACING THE WORLD

I cannot say at what point I crossed over from the brink of spiritual death, to the desire for spiritual life. All I knew was that I was an altered person with a journey under my belt that had changed me forever. I was by no means suddenly healed, but finally on the way to accepting the fact that I had to live, more than live, I had to grow and blossom.

Neither can I say at what point I decided to leave my marriage and never return. It was more a natural outgrowth of the preceding events rather than a deliberate decision. Growing and blossoming was something I was never going to be able to do if I continued to deny myself or how I really felt. Forcing myself to be something I am not, feel something I cannot feel out of guilt or to make another person happy, is itself a death, and I wanted to live. I did not want to die.

It was time for me to leave my old life and be willing to build a new one. I began a series of actions, determined not to squash myself anymore. Somehow I knew I was going to be okay, even though I had no inkling of where I was going, or what my life would be like when I got there.

I drove one last time to the women's group, nervously contemplating how I was going to say I was leaving my husband, Suzie and the group. I asked God to help me choose words that were grounded and self-assured. I wanted to appear strong and in charge, even though on the inside I was quivering in fear at the prospect of standing up to such a powerful woman. I knew it was not going to go down well.

By the time we were in our circle and it came my turn to speak, I was no longer afraid, but settled and calm. I told the women how much I'd come to love and value them. They would always be my sisters, but it was time for me to move on. I needed to throw off the shroud of my childhood and release the weight of a painful marriage. I was tired of the constant feeling of being lifeless. The room went deadly quiet, and Suzie was visibly caught off guard.

I went on to say I wanted to grow beyond the disempowered life I lived. Turning to Suzie, I thanked her for the time and effort she'd put into being my counsellor and went on to talk about my desire to find a brighter, happier life, beyond all the heaviness and sorrow. I wanted to let go of my fear of the world and have a look at what might be out there for me. I was making a bid for the right to govern my own life, free from the fear of being wrong all the time, and free from the fear of punishment for displeasing other people.

Suzie's eyes darted from face to face around the circle; looking to see what impact my words were having on the others. She was afraid my leaving the fold in such a self-confident and self-supporting way, might inspire others to believe in themselves and follow suit. Immediately she went into damage control.

Suzie asked for a right to reply and I told her I welcomed her thoughts, bracing myself for what her steely brown eyes told me was coming. Her sting was condemning. I was selfish and thoughtless. I was letting the women down by not being loyal and committed to the group, and I had no right to leave my husband and take his children away from him. If anyone else had any ideas about leaving anytime soon, they were squashed.

Following Suzie's admonishment, the women were invited to take turns in sharing their thoughts about what I was doing. The majority seemed respectful of my decision and cautiously wished me well, not wanting to appear to be approving, but the woman on my left began to cry and shake uncontrollably, un-nerving everyone's composure. The part of her that was fearful of embracing her own adult woman power was noticeably shrinking back in her chair, making her look like a small child recoiling from something too terrible to contemplate. In her opinion I was deceiving myself and ultimately walking into all sorts of evil danger. Suzie took the opportunity to let the women know they were right where they needed to be, working with the bravery I clearly didn't have.

At the end of the night we all hugged goodbye and I keenly felt the distance between myself and the women I'd been so close to over so many months. I was no longer one of them, but a deserter. Saving Suzie for last, I put my arms around her and hugged her close, intentionally putting as much affection and warmth as I could into my embrace. I did not want to leave with powerless blame, but with empowered self-responsibility. Good or bad, Suzie had been a teacher of lessons.

I told my husband I wanted a divorce. Each time I'd left our marriage previously, I'd gone secretively, leaving him to come home to a deserted house. I'd been too scared to stand up to him and stay strong in the face of his fear, anger and pain. It always managed to take priority over me in the end. This time, I had the courage to face him directly. He knew it was over for good.

I moved into our study, turning the little room into a sanctuary. I put my few special things and books on a shelf, set up my C.D. player, and soothed myself at night with relaxation music. It was such a relief to be free from the issue of sex. The discomfort of sleeping on our old couch was worth the ache in my back, a small price to pay. I wanted only to belong to myself.

Towards the end of our deteriorating marriage and while still working with Suzie, I'd used guided meditation tapes to try and help me reconnect to spirit. Surprisingly, I'd learnt instead to become so relaxed that a world of peaceful space opened to me. There were no boundaries, no walls or confines as I travelled the quiet within. I could become completely unaware I even had a body and be only the rhythm of my exquisite breath.

On one occasion, I dropped into that space and felt the centre of my forehead tingle. It had happened before, but this time the feeling of stillness that came over me was pure bliss. Basking in this sensation, I understood that if I had peace in God within as a living part of who I am, it would not matter if I were a beggar on the street sleeping only on the ground, because the feeling of connection, the serenity, would make me the richest person on earth. Anything that happened to my body was irrelevant. Beyond it was encompassing love.

Sadly, I'd stopped stealing that time for myself as my marriage fell apart, becoming instead, embroiled in the hostilities. I missed those quiet times. Now, all I wanted was to find my way back in, hoping those moments of peace would carry me through the days and weeks ahead. I spent time alone desperately trying to reconnect, but constant, fearful thinking had again taken over.

I still cooked and cleaned but refused to do my husband's room or his laundry, making him angrier. He felt it was still my responsibility. For me, it was a statement that we were separate people who were no longer in a marriage. I didn't want to do personal things for him. I knew if I did, I'd lose the division I'd claimed for my emerging self. Our fighting escalated as my unavailability to my husband's demands became clearer.

In desperation I attended a meditation course, hoping to find answers and the presence of Spirit. But the course was immensely frustrating. I wasn't experiencing anything and felt stupid when others said they were having elaborate visionary journeys, traversing the universe on the back of a dragon or some other mythical creature. I was considering pulling out when the woman running the group suggested a change in routine. We were to have a go at feeling each other's' energy fields with our hands.

I baulked at the idea. It sounded too airy-fairy to me. As I suspected, I couldn't feel a thing, while others were getting excited saying they could feel tingles in their hands. I thought we all looked rather ridiculous passing our hands up and down each other's bodies trying to sense something we couldn't see.

That night, while drying one of my sons after his bath, I decided to have another go. I was curious and felt more comfortable doing it without anyone watching. I shut the bathroom door so I wouldn't be seen, put my right hand on my son's tummy and used the palm of my left hand to slowly pass up and down his back, starting at his head and moving down toward his feet.

Relaxed and not feeling pressure to achieve anything, I went quiet within myself. As I passed my hand continually up and down his spine, I felt three areas in my son's back that gave off a sensation of prickly heat, and somehow, I knew he had three disks misaligned in his back.

The following morning, I took my son to see the therapist I went to for spinal manipulation. Not wanting to appear silly, I didn't tell him what I thought I'd found. Sure enough, my son had only been on the table a few minutes when Ron declared he'd found three protruding disks. They were exactly where I'd felt the heat. I marvelled at how I'd felt it.

Back in my sanctuary, I continued to battle hard with myself, not wanting to waiver in my decision to leave my marriage. I'd come and gone through fear, guilt and manipulation, been in and out of counselling, twisted myself into every conceivable shape, and taken the heat for others' behaviours and faults as well as my own. I'd opened myself up as best I could to make my marriage work, but it always seemed to come at a price. My own extinction.

Whenever I felt myself begin to doubt my justifications for leaving, I would go over in my mind all the loveless things done to the children and myself over the years. There were incidents that stood out, events that bit by bit had killed off any feelings of love I might have had for my husband. Like the two occasions he left bruises on our daughter's arm after using her to vent his aggravations. It was repellent and something I never expected to see.

Once, while violently ill from a bad bout of food poisoning, I was left all day unable to care for myself, let alone two, on-the-run toddlers. I couldn't eat, drink or walk. My husband had refused to stay home to look after them, instead insisting on going to get a trailer-load of second-hand bricks from a building site he thought were too good to pass up. While he was gone, I virtually had to crawl along the floor to get to where I needed to go, be it the toilet or do what needed to be done for the boys. I felt abandoned, unimportant and unworthy of care.

On another occasion I'd again been left alone, only this time for two days, shut off in our bedroom at the far end of the house after being misdiagnosed at our local hospital. I had severe pelvic pain and was barely able to move, yet still expected to look after our toddlers as normal. It was the weekend and my husband had his usual jobs list he wanted to get through outside, so he was extremely annoyed at having to be the one to look after them when I insisted I couldn't manage.

From the other side of our bedroom door, I could hear my sons being scolded harshly by their father as the first day slipped by, his voice impatient and unkind. They cried a lot and my heart went out to them. I tried to call out to my husband, but he either didn't hear me or chose not to respond. The hours dragged on and I dozed in between increasingly uncomfortable bouts of nausea and vomiting. I hadn't eaten or had any fluids, so all I was bringing up was bile and bubbly froth.

The nausea became acute, coming in intensely unbearable, rolling waves. Unable to move I tried to call out again, but my voice was weak, and the house was so quiet I thought it empty. My husband never came to check on me or offer me a glass of water over the two days. I was being punished for the inconvenience of him being saddled with our children.

By the end of the second day, I'd become so ill, the nausea and dry retching so severe, it was difficult to get through the heaving and keep breathing at the same time. Realising I was in serious trouble and on my own, I managed to reach the cordless telephone on the bedside table and call my GP. Her advice was to call an ambulance.

It was dark when it arrived. I could hear the ambulance drivers banging on our front door, and the shocked tone of my husband's voice as he directed them to me. When the bedroom door finally opened, I grasped at the two men, begging them to knock me out. I was in such agony I couldn't cope any more. It was a petrifying experience. The concerned husband act that followed as I was taken out on a stretcher, left me cold.

Once back at the hospital, it became clear my left ovary had ruptured and I'd haemorrhaged internally. I was also severely dehydrated, which is why the nausea and dry retching had been so relentless.

Even as I remembered these things, telling myself it was okay to feel angry and let down, I would sit with the Bible or other spiritual books in my hands, and tear myself apart over my terror that I was simply being selfish. Without the sureness of knowing if I was right or wrong in feeling the way I did, I was at the mercy of crushing fear and guilt.

One of the books was *A Course in Miracles*. Asking for guidance, I opened it to a random page and read a paragraph. It said that in any troubled relationship, no matter how we have judged another to be wrong because of our perception of fear instead of love, we can invite the presence of the Holy Spirit into the union, asking that all misperceptions be healed. Then it was a matter of waiting on the power of God to make the necessary corrections, in his time, not ours. I shut the book quickly. My truth was that I really didn't want to stay.

I remembered the ridicule from my husband after I'd asked him for space from the pressure of sex when I first began to address my sexual abuse issues. I'd needed time to repossess my body as my own, wanting only to find a place in myself that was able to give freely and without obligation or duty. My body had never been my own and I wanted to claim it back, but he'd reacted with anger, saying I'd let my uncle do it, so he should be able to, too. What was he supposed to do with his dick, put it in a drawer for the duration?

I recalled many instances of hurt and the controlling ways in which my husband manipulated. And I felt the accumulated bitterness because of the way he took his anger and frustration out on our children to punish me. I held on to it all, trying to reassure myself I had a right to feel the way I did.

On the other occasions I'd left my marriage, guilt and a belief in my lack of entitlement would not allow me to consider taking a settlement. In fact, I'd promised my husband I would let him keep everything. He'd constantly reminded me how devastated he'd be if he ever lost anything, and would lament the financial setback of his first divorce. The material possessions we'd accumulated throughout our life together, the big house, the nice furniture and the two cars, combined as the sum of what he'd worked for since. It was how he valued and measured himself.

As far as he was concerned, the fact that I was leaving him meant I forfeited any rights to his possessions. I could leave, but not take anything with me. After all, I'd been just a barmaid when we met. If it were not for him, I would still be roaming the countryside.

This time however, I knew I had to establish security for my children and myself. I'd also grown enough to understand I'd worked just as hard as he and in fact, it was I who'd been instrumental in getting him off the tools and into a suit and tie with a pay packet beyond anything he'd ever had before. I'd also worked outside the home when I'd been allowed. I had a right to a share of what we'd created together as a couple.

At the same time our marriage ended, so did our plastics fabrication business. The debt with the Taxation Department had accumulated to the extent they were no longer prepared to give us time to pay. They demanded the debt be settled or they would take our house and put us out on the street. As directors of the company, we were liable.

When evaluating and discussing what I was entitled to by way of settlement, my husband almost had a seizure. I got to see the fullness of his nasty side, because now it had come down to money, and everything we had, he considered his. I was shocked to see it emerge to the extent it did.

Everything was falling around him. I came up with what I thought was a fair figure, no more than half of what I believed the house to be worth, but as far as he was concerned, I was not entitled to much. He wanted me to foot the bill for half the Tax debt.

I was furious. When I'd begged my husband to listen to my concerns about the business, I was dismissed, disrespected and devalued. I lived in his house, cooked, cleaned and provided services, but I was not even remotely an equal partner. Now he wanted to bring me into the mess and use me to save himself as much money as possible. It was irrelevant what it would do to me, or how it would affect my ability to care for our children. He'd gambled with our lives and valued his long association with his friend more than the wellbeing of his own wife and family. As far as I was concerned, he and the manager should stand up and take responsibility for their actions. I was not going to suffer the liability for something I'd had no choice in.

I pushed through his verbal mauling and held my ground. After months of battling through lawyers, I received my half of the value of our house in a cash settlement, and left. Throughout that process, it became clear my husband had financial secrets he didn't want my lawyer or me to delve into.

When I left, I took a new set of beliefs about myself with me. "I am incapable of love," and "Something is wrong with me". Those beliefs were okay with me. All I wanted was to find somewhere quiet so I could mend. I felt broken, afraid and fragile.

I found a small house to buy, not too far away so my children could have easy access to their father, and he to them. My guilt and sense of shared parenting wouldn't allow me to put much distance between them. I bought an old car that was in reasonable condition and gave the good one I drove back to my husband. I was not allowed to take anything other than the essentials out of the house. The high-quality furniture my husband valued was not to be touched. Watching over me and the removalist, he made it perfectly clear if I was to try to take any of it, he'd knock my head off my shoulders. With the remainder of the money I bought enough cheap furniture to cover what we needed.

Once all was settled and the children and I were organised in our new home, I collapsed with fatigue. There was so much ahead to deal with; the distressing experiences of the years and subsequent emotional turmoil to process. We had all been through a devastating time.

I had to work through the aftermath and address my share of the responsibility for the wounding our children suffered, but I also had to carry my husband's. He very neatly packaged it up and handed it over to me. I was solely to blame. I took the package and buckled under the weight.

I had to face my fear of growing up, and consider how I was going to support myself and my family now I no longer had a husband to depend on. My only immediate option was to go on the single parent pension, but it made me feel like a freeloader. The pension also meant the government system dictated my life. I still was not free. There was maintenance to negotiate and more power-play, blackmail and bullying over that.

The ongoing nasty conflict over money didn't end there. My husband showed up at my house, wanting me to sign some legal documents accepting half the Tax dept from the business, even though it had been written into our marriage settlement that he agreed to take full responsibility for it in return for my resignation as silent Director of his company.

When I refused, stressing I'd lose the house I'd just purchased and come out of it with nothing, he became aggressive and verbally abusive. Frightened and unsure of how far he might go, I pushed the kids inside the house and demanded he leave. I was stunned. He really didn't care about what happened to us at all.

During our first year, the Department of Social Security cut off my pension without warning. I wasn't receiving the amount of maintenance they told me I had to have based on my husband's income. We'd come to a private deal we thought was reasonable. I felt bad and didn't want to place my husband under additional financial stress. Our agreement had been incorporated into our marriage settlement via the Family Law Court. Neither of us knew it held no weight with the Social Security system if you were a welfare recipient.

Social Security, having no legal recourse with my husband, went through me to try to force him to pay the increased amount they insisted on. It became a battle with my husband and his threats on one side, and Social Security with theirs on the other. It was a terrifying experience. I was caught between two forces that had rule over my interests. I could not see how I was ever going to be free and not controlled or dictated to by the power and authority of either. Nor could I figure out who was the bigger thug, my husband or Social Security. I didn't know how to satisfy the demands or intimidations from either of them. Eventually, after much hardship it was settled, and we fell into a more financially stable time.

I also had to grieve the loss of my marriage. There was the letting go process to move through, the death of a dream to have a happy family life with a happy ending. I was the one who left, but I still grieved its passing.

Even though my husband was at times not the nicest person to be married to, I was far from blameless. We each had histories that affected our ability to have a healthy relationship. While my husband had his faults, I too, had mine and had hurt him with my own behaviour as our marriage wore on.

Each time I'd left he'd taken me back, paid my bills, and did the best he could the only way he knew how. After each event occurred, three times in as many years, he'd tried to be a better husband and towards the end, he'd stretched himself in his effort to save our marriage. However, I was emotionally erratic and as changeable as the wind.

During the latter years, there had been moments when I'd looked at my husband with warmth, feeling a rush of love. They were precious windows that opened where I felt light and free. I'd walk up behind him at a market stall or shop, kiss his cheek from the side or on the back of his neck, and whisper in his ear that I loved him.

Rare moments of peace being a normal family strolling in a garden nursery on a Sunday morning, gave me relief from the compressed world I lived in. At other times, I hated my husband for being a man and despised him for wanting me. But it was over now, really over. Slowly, tentatively, I attempted to re-build my life.

At age four my sons started pre-primary. The impact on them of being in an unstable home situation with volatile and emotionally unavailable parents was glaringly obvious. Both boys had disturbing behaviours preventing them from being able to fit in with a group.

It had already been in the back of my mind for some time that my boys, like their sister, might also have ADD, only with hyperactivity. She was the quiet dreamer type, while they were always full-throttle and making mischief. I'd been told if both parents had the condition, it was a certainty all children from that union would have it. I didn't want it to be true, even more, I didn't want to create a self-fulfilling prophesy for them, so I tried not to think about it.

My daughter was unable to settle into our little house. She was racked with concern for her father, and she and I constantly fought. All her hurt and anger was directed exclusively at me. In her mind everything was my fault and I was the only one to blame. I didn't know it at the time, but her father had told her stories about me in secret conversations, covertly drawing her in and making her feel responsible for his feelings. She had every right to feel distraught, and out of fear and confusion was unable to express any of it to her father.

Living together cooped up with our significant distress and insecurity became too much to cope with. After uselessly screaming at my children as they ran wild fighting and arguing with each other, I'd often slide down the wall to the floor while they verbally tore each other apart. All I could do was watch from my position on the floor and think, "My God! What have I done?"

There was no mending my relationship with my daughter. It had been too badly damaged. She also had intense issues about her brothers, making it impossible for us to be together without constant hostility and recriminations. Equally, they set out to upset her. We lived in deeply wounded chaos trying to find something to hold on to. Riddled with shame and blame, I couldn't help any of us. Within a matter of months my daughter moved back to live with her father, bringing the prophecy of the broken crystal to life. It had come down to my sons and me on one side, and my husband with our daughter on the other.

My daughter moving out gave us breathing space from each other and made things more manageable with the twins. It was hard to let her go, but at thirteen she was angry, adamant and bitter, and I didn't know what else to do.

Now I was alone with two boys who were destructive and hyperactive, keeping me in a constant state of hyper-vigilance to protect them from themselves and each other. I felt weighed down by the responsibility of being the cause of all their problems, and hid myself at home in shame, trying to keep our dysfunction from the eyes of the world. But we couldn't go on that way. I was out of my depth and unable to fix anything on my own. I had to address the issue and be willing to explore other possibilities. I went back into counselling with a new therapist, before taking them to a paediatrician on her recommendation.

By the time my sons were a quarter of the way through pre-school, they were diagnosed as having Attention Deficit Hyperactivity Disorder, and put on medication just as their sister had been. More guilt and shame followed. I was a complete failure at being able to make everything right. It crushed me further down in my estimations of myself.

After some initial trial and error finding the right medication for each boy and juggling dosages, our lives became more manageable, with periods of respite and peace. There were no doubts the tablets had an effect.

Putting my boys on medication twisted my insides. I felt I was feeding them poison, but it had come down to salvaging my sanity, and our survival as a family. The hardest part was getting used to the Clonidine, a medication used to put them to sleep at night. One of my sons would go into such a deep sleep, I was terrified he'd stop breathing. I'd sit on the floor beside him and watch his chest move until I pass out. There wasn't anything about our lives that felt safe.

For the next two years I spent what money I could spare on trying different natural therapies to replace the tablets, but it became too hard to keep coming up with the cash for expensive products, and too hard to maintain the faith to keep trying. Most of the time I felt beaten. I was damned if I did and damned if I didn't medicate.

Both boys later had assessments at the Curtin University Psychology Clinic and were found to have problems with learning in maths and reading. I sometimes wondered if being sick, premature IVF babies, could have been partly responsible.

In that same first two years I lived in dread of receiving mail, terrified something would come to snatch away the freedom I was trying to establish. Any letter from Social Security had me trembling. My heart would pound and the familiar restriction in my chest would rob me of my breath. I still had big issues with not feeling safe, fearing any threat could take me down. It was a slow process to build any sense of trust that the world could be a safe place.

The only way I coped with all the feelings I had, the guilt, shame, low self-worth and inadequacies as a parent, was to shut down emotionally. I had no support, no friends, and no skills to deal with life or my boys' behaviours. I began to take it out on them. Both suffered at my hand at different times and both cowered on the floor in fear of me when I lashed out with verbal rage.

My heart went dead. I couldn't feel for them. When they were hurting emotionally, crying and in need of me and I was in that frame of mind, my words spat at them through clenched teeth. Sometimes I'd pace the floor like a wild animal in a cage, completely at my wits' end, wondering how to make it all stop.

Underpinning all of it was fear, huge terrifying fear. I was afraid I was insane, afraid of my children and their issues, and afraid of myself because there were times when I was out of control. I tried to get help, but because of the age of my boys, limited and inadequate resources in the public health care system, we continually fell through not just cracks, but huge gaps in services. Not knowing what else to do I gave up. Behind closed doors we blundered through the misery on our own, living a distressing life.

While the boys were at school I thought about what I could do to get back into the workforce. I had no qualifications or skills that were of any value to anyone. Right from the start I put myself under enormous pressure about finding a way to support myself and my family, when what I really needed to do was let go, rest, sleep and heal. I couldn't just be still. If it wasn't my body moving, it was my mind going round and round in endless circles of anxious thinking.

I really had no idea what I was capable of, or what it was I wanted to do. Even though I'd taken an IQ test after my ADD diagnosis, revealing my place in the top twenty-five percent of the population, I still feared I was dumb, that somehow, I'd fluked the results.

At the time, putting myself through the test was intensely challenging. It felt like I was exposing myself to something that could have a catastrophic outcome if it went badly.

But I was desperate to know, once and for all, if I was something other than simply stupid. When the educational psychologist phoned the following night with my results, she said I would have scored much higher if I hadn't been so stressed about taking it.

Throughout my marriage I frequently expressed to my husband a desire to go back to school. I was interested in welfare work. Just as the idea of me having a job outside the home, the subject was always met with anger and conflict. As far as my husband was concerned, if I'd wanted to learn I should have done it while I was at school, or before I married him. If I insisted on working, I should become a secretary. They were paid more, and didn't bring home all that unpleasant stuff welfare workers got involved in.

I'd tried to explain that because of the environment I grew up in, I hadn't been able to learn. It was not something I willingly chose for myself. Besides, I didn't want to be a secretary. I wanted to work helping other people and I didn't care how much money it paid. It wasn't about the money, it was about contribution and meaningful participation. I always lost the arguments.

Something inside me was hungry. I wanted to learn, to know about the world. Inside I felt a huge vacancy of knowledge, a cavity that lacked comprehension about people, life, and how it all worked. I was looking to become part of it, just like everybody else.

Once, without telling my husband, I enrolled in an English course at TAFE. On my first day, I stood in the doorway of the classroom, seeing first the lecturer, then the students. Gripped by panic, my face flushed crimson as I unexpectedly flashed back to my schooldays as a child. Embarrassed and unable to enter the room, I ran back to my car and drove home in tears.

Later, after leaving my marriage the second time, I'd again made a bid to learn and grow, enrolling in TAFE to study Human Services at a part-time workload. But nothing about me was cohesive. The twins were only two years old and I was living with complete craziness, taking dexamphetamine for ADD and Prozac for mental exhaustion and depression. Between the pills and not being able to sleep, I was spinning out of control psychologically. Unable to cope, I gave up after completing only the first term.

While thinking about my situation now, it occurred to me that my circumstances were considerably different. I was no longer on medication and hadn't been since the incident in the bottom of the shower. I was readier than I'd ever been to go back to TAFE and complete what I'd started. I still had my books and letter of results showing the modules I'd passed stashed away in a box of useless dreams. Again, I enrolled in the Human Services course, this time throwing myself in with sheer delight and enthusiasm.

I loved being in the classroom and loved the process of learning. It made me feel alive. Finally, I began to get a taste of what I'd missed out on. Feeling grown-up and in charge of my future, I bought a modest computer to do my assignments on.

But as the course progressed I unexpectedly found myself becoming disillusioned. Somehow I'd managed to retain a certain naiveté, and had trusted what I would learn would fill in the gaps in my understanding, but it didn't. Instead, it showed me government policies and systems only put Band-Aids on our social problems, and people's lives.

Learning the basics of how government operated and what their priorities were, also showed me many organisations set up to help people in crisis, existed precariously on limited funding they continually had to fight and scratch for to keep running. They often had their hands tied behind their backs and achieved little real change. It would have been overwhelmingly frustrating for me to be involved in such a system. I didn't want to tie myself up with more bonds after having struggled so hard to free myself of the ones I'd had.

My experiences had created a vastly distinct perspective, one that didn't fit with the mainstream. I now came from a more spiritual perception. Both realities were at odds with each other, and I didn't know how to marry them together. It made me feel just as much an alien on a strange planet as I had before, but this time for a different reason.

Unable to reconcile my changed awareness with how the world functions, I decided to run away, not wanting to be a part of it and its illogical ways. Nothing about it made sense to me. I quit TAFE four units short of completing my certificate and did a Swedish massage course instead, with the intention of starting a small business from home. I could hide away from the rest of the world. I also decided I could legitimately use it to explore my ability to feel energy with my hands. As I opened myself to it, I discovered I could do hands-on healing.

In the beginning it was particularly strong, and I used it on family and friends with seemingly miraculous results. During a healing, all I had to do was open my heart to the love and presence of the divine, and healing would occur. I understood the Source was pure and free from any human belief or teaching.

When my mother had a migraine, I would place my hands around her head, and within minutes it would be gone, yet I was riddled with self-doubt. I couldn't just accept the result. I'd ask who ever I was healing if the pain was really gone, or if they were just saying it to humour me. I would follow up with more questions, wanting to know every few minutes if their pain had returned, trying to gauge if the healing was fake, or at best, a short-term occurrence.

Not knowing anything about hands-on healing, I attended a Conscious Living Expo looking for something that would help me understand how to work with it, but much of what I saw made me uncomfortable. All I could see were the sales pitches and props people used to attract the would-be client. The lashings of purple, the strange names of channelled beings, the brightly coloured cards of those professing to hold the answers to another's journey, and the elaborate rituals and myriad beliefs underpinning much of the New Age movement. It seemed wrong somehow, something I didn't want to be a part of. Everything in me screamed for simplicity. To me, all the external paraphernalia detracted from the true power and purity of the Source and weakened its potency, if it was present at all.

Going to the Expo deepened my inner conflict. While doing healings, I experienced something so profoundly simple and boundless, it filled me with reverent awe, but I just couldn't comprehend how that kind of extraordinary Grace could come through me, when I had done nothing to deserve it.

The bottom line was, regardless of the results I got, somehow it was a mistake. It was a gift given to the wrong person. I was again an imposter, struggling to understand the how and why of it, or what I was supposed to do with it. But by far, my greatest concern was that my unseen, dirty contamination, could somehow inadvertently be passed through to others. It plagued my conscience until in the end, it was impossible to override. I stopped being willing to do healings at all.

I continued to work at becoming established in massage. I offered my services free to the clients of a local women's centre. I felt unworthy of charging a fee, but as the months passed, I grew a little in confidence and eventually charged ten dollars a massage. Later, I cautiously put it up to fifteen.

Initially my ability to stay in one place was sorely tested. I couldn't stay present or focused for longer than five minutes let alone an hour, which is how long it takes to complete a basic massage session. Confined in a smallish room I felt trapped and edgy. The minutes ticked by incredibly slow. My thoughts frequently shifted from one worrying concern to another, and the negative voice in my head constantly pulled me down. It said I was no good at anything and I had no right to even try. I could never be respectable or accomplished in any area of my life. By the time

I finished my second client I'd be stressing about how long it was going to be before I could go home. I was constantly squirming.

I knew I had a problem with being centred and present for the person I was working with, so I resolved to train myself out of it. Each time I became aware my mind had wandered into fear and panic, I would force my attention back my client and what I was doing. Perseverance and determination gradually began to pay off.

My room was set up with an oil burner, candles and peaceful relaxation music intended to be soothing aesthetics for my clients, but I discovered a balm for my own soul. The music became one of my main tools for learning to feel soft, breathe more freely, and open to my feelings.

With patience and practice, the massage sessions began to flow more smoothly, and I grew to love the work. There was something beautiful about massage. It was like a ballet. My hands were the dancers and the body the stage. It became a form of meditation for me.

Once I'd developed enough confidence, I took the next step and started taking clients at home, only going to the women's centre one day a week. I charged the new price of twenty-five dollars a massage, but still felt hugely guilty and uncomfortable about taking money for my work.

Distracted by what I was trying to achieve, my boys, worries and daily life in general, I didn't realise my weight was increasing. Something in my body was changing. I couldn't remember who I had been, did not know who I was now, or who I was becoming. Nothing in my wardrobe fitted anymore, my hair had grown long covering much of my face, and I'd had my nose pierced.

With the changes to my life, my body and my identity, I felt cloaked, hooded somehow. I'd sit in my kitchen staring out the window for hours, not knowing who I was, how I felt, or how to join the world. I didn't know how to dress, what clothes I liked, what looked good, what looked bad, or how to be comfortable with myself.

Sometimes I would cry, sometimes I would talk to God. Mostly I sat in quiet emptiness, my emotions swinging from sadness, loss and regret, to hopeful plans with reflections of trust whenever I managed to remember Spirit was with me somewhere. But I never at any time sank back into the deep despair I'd known before. On some level I understood what I was going through was part of grieving my old life, the end of my marriage, and my fear of being alone.

My bulimia resurfaced, and I was once again wrestling daily with feelings of vile fullness in my body. After its long absence, it was agonising to be going through the violence that came with forced purging. I felt like I was choking on myself. It made my head thump and my eyes sting.

Bulimia was so incompatible with the person I wanted to be. It seemed so much more intolerable than I'd remembered. I couldn't stand it. One afternoon I refused to give into the agitation and urge to purge. I took myself to my room and sat on the edge of my bed instead. Placing one hand on my forehead and the other at the base of the back of my head, I centred myself and focused on my breathing. It was a technique I'd been told was useful for calming fear.

Within seconds an image of me as a little girl came into my mind. She was kneeling on the ground with her head over a bucket, heaving and heaving her small frame. I watched and held the image, felt the bile rise in my mouth, the contractions of my stomach tighten and release with each new wave as she spewed relentlessly into the bucket, until I was exhausted, having released the energy completely from my body. When it was over, I realised I had been holding the unexpressed revulsion my inner child carried about the things that had been done to her. My bulimia had been a manifestation of an unconscious need to vomit up my childhood.

One morning soon after, while getting ready to go to the centre, I walked past my bathroom door and caught a side-line glimpse of myself in the mirror. The shock of what I saw jerked me to a stunned halt. I hadn't recognised the person walking.

I took a backward step, stood in the doorway and stared at my reflection. I studied my face, my hair, and my body. I took out my nose stud, decided to cut my hair and clear my face, and made a commitment to go back and get me, wherever I was.

My resolution to get myself together soon wore off. I was feeling bulky, bloated and toxic. I had pain in my pelvis and was sweating profusely. It didn't dawn on me I was sick until I realised the pain I was having in my back was coming from my left kidney. I kept working. I had a high tolerance for pain, pelvic pain particularly, but the kidney pain was different, and it got worse.

Pushing on was typical. I was just like my mother, a Clydesdale horse that could keep going. I was strong even when I was weak. I pushed through pain to show how indomitable I was, just like my mother. She had suffered, endured, kept on going because she had to. So could I.

However, this time I couldn't push through the pain. I went to my doctor. After some investigation, it was discovered my left ovary was the size of a tennis ball with a mass of endometrial growths, and it was pressing against my urinary tract. As a result, my kidney was backed up and not working properly.

Endometriosis wasn't new to me. I'd been plagued with pain and 'women's troubles' since the birth of my first child, coinciding with the emergence of my childhood history. Over the later years, haemorrhagic cysts bled into my pelvis, and the bleeding made sense to me. I long ago described in journal writings the feeling of dying I lived with as a perpetual state of slowly bleeding to death. I had learnt enough to know it was an expression of my history, the sexual abuse from my past, and my unconscious rejection of my female body.

I'd wanted a hysterectomy for a long time, but my doctor kept holding off for as long as possible. There was never any guarantee having my uterus and ovaries removed would solve my problems. But at last the time had come. I was sick of the constant pain and period problems, the heavy bleeding, cramps and inconvenience.

I couldn't wait to get on the table. I imagined the surgeon cutting out the blackness that swamped the cells in that part of my body. If he took everything, the past would be taken too. I wanted it all cut out.

The operation went well, but I was told the surgeon had not taken my right ovary. There'd been no need as it was unaffected by the cysts. My first reaction was one of anger; it disturbed me to think something female remained functioning in my body. I wanted to be castrated, sexless, and free from all the blackness.

The first night following surgery, I had a nightmare relating to my family and sexual abuse. It was sickening. I woke nauseated and distressed. The hysterectomy triggered gruesome unconscious gunge that bubbled and gurgled its way to the surface. I had similar nightmares each night following until I left the hospital.

I had firmly believed, prior to the operation, I would have no issue with grief or any emotion relating to the removal of my uterus. I believed I would be fine and free at last. I was released from the hospital four days after the surgery. My children were staying with their father for two weeks to give me time to recuperate, and I went to a friend's place for the first week.

I left the hospital with clear instructions not to drive for seven days. My friend drove me to her house where my car was waiting for when I was able. But the need to be alone was gnawing at my insides, and after less than twenty-four hours, I got in my car and cautiously drove myself home. It was heaven to be in silence in my own place. I revelled in the quiet for a couple of hours, then got back in my car to return to my friend.

It was a lovely sunny afternoon. The heat of the day radiated through my windscreen wrapping me in a cosy blanket of warmth. The birds were singing and everything seemed beautiful and tranquil. Pulling out from a side street after looking left, I dreamily entered a dual carriageway that had two lanes of traffic going up a hill, and two lanes going down towards the city. Intending to turn right I put my foot on the accelerator and nudged out into the road. Immediately a voice in my head said, "You forgot to look right."

My head snapped around just in time to see two cars coming down the hill about to smash into me. In that split-second I saw it all, where the cars would hit and which car would hit me first. In an instant I braked, the outside car veered around me shooting off over the medium strip into oncoming traffic on the other side of the road. I accelerated in a surge forward to just miss the car in the lane closest to me. That one swerved around the other end of me, slamming on its brakes and coming to rest on the footpath metres further down the road. Billowing white smoke and the sound of screeching tyres filled the air. The sickening noise shocked me back to reality.

Once safely on the other side of the carriageway, heading in the direction I needed to go, I slowed down but didn't stop. My heart was thumping like a sledgehammer as I checked in my rear-vision mirror to see if the people in the two cars were okay. Thankfully they appeared to have escaped unharmed.

Whispering a prayer of thanks, I kept driving, too scared to face the consequences of my actions. I knew what I'd done was reckless and dangerous. I vowed never to do anything so stupid again. My belly was full of fresh stitches, my body still processing all the morphine and pethidine I'd had, as well as the effects of the anaesthetic. I had no business being on the road.

When the week came to an end I went home, grateful to be back in my own bed. The drugs had well and truly worn off, allowing me to feel the hollow space in my belly where my uterus had been. The sensation caused enormous agitation, a writhing unease and anger I systematically shoved down as much as I could. But it soon became apparent I wasn't going to be able to ignore it. In the end, I had to acknowledge how I was feeling.

One night I ran a hot bath and prepared it with oils. Candles provided comforting soft light, and low soothing music from my faithful C.D. player filled the small bathroom. Gratefully I lowered my body into the water, feeling myself submerge into the warmth, closing my eyes to the world as I went. It was so good to just stop and be; something I'd not done for some time.

My intention was to simply relax and meditate on acceptance so I could give myself some relief, but the minute I let go, all the suppressed emotion and denied squirming in my belly erupted from the depths with a howl that reverberated off the four walls. I felt like a gutted she-wolf howling at the moon. The intensity was frightening.

Guttural noises echoed in the bathroom, scaring me with the sound of its pain, but it was coming from me. All I could do was sob, feel, surrender to the loss of my womanhood, my youth, and realise the expression of ritual as I passed from one stage of woman-life into another. But it was not a natural passing, it was a butchered passing and it broke my heart.

For the longest time I felt tender and vulnerable, but what was done couldn't be undone. As soon as I was able, I went back to my massage work trying to pick up from where I'd left off, but everything had changed. I needed to start all over again.

I didn't want to go back to the women's centre. I was keen to have a go at building a regular client base from home. I had my lounge/dining area modified by adding an extra wall and door, creating a space for myself to use as a work room. I made my own business cards and advertised in the local paper.

Working at home, I was at peace developing a deeper connection with my clients, and could relax and enjoy the experience much more. My clients were teaching me not to be so afraid of people, gently helping me overcome my profound sense of disconnection to, and fear of others.

I only worked with women. I had too many un-healed issues to work with men. It was a scary and threatening prospect, but I knew eventually I would have to deal with it, and that came around soon enough. Each time I advertised in the local paper offering my services to women only, men would respond, and in every instance they wanted sexual favours. I would remove the ads feeling repulsed and angry.

In time, some of my clients began sending their husbands for a massage, giving me an opportunity to face my fears. I felt secure knowing they were someone's partner and not a sleaze seeking sexual services.

Slowly I progressed to being willing to weed out the genuine calls from men, but one managed to slip through, ending up in my home and on my table. Rather than be afraid, I handled it by consciously working through my issues and deliberately giving the most loving, nurturing massage I could possibly give. He left in tears.

Once I realised it was time to stop responding from a wounded place, and without judgment, simply and respectfully making clear my boundaries, I began to feel safe. When I received obvious phone calls, I kindly gave another number for them to ring instead of hurling scathing abuse down the mouthpiece. I knew it was something I'd finally cleared when I stopped receiving those types of calls altogether. Life reflects our fears and beliefs by bringing them in for us to deal with, plain and simple.

I began to have intuitive insights into the personal growth of the people I was massaging. I could perceive hidden trapped emotions in the tissue of their bodies. Sometimes I had pictorial impressions that transferred understanding without words. I would be able to relate back to my clients where they were stuck and what they could do to move past it. It was common to feel the company of Spirit in the room, and sometimes people received healing.

I was in the shower one afternoon, thinking about my work and feeling a deep sense of awe for the extraordinary intelligence that our bodies have, when suddenly I became aware of my hands. Lathering them with soap I recognised I was consciously feeling and appreciating them in a way I never had before. It was a bittersweet moment.

The beautiful sensations on my skin made me cry. I held my hands up to the sunlight coming through the bathroom window and studied them, mesmerised by their simplicity, struck by the things they could accomplish. I thought about God and marvelled at the holy presence that lives within and around us. I moved my hands up to my arms and gently traced soapy fingers along their length. I cried as I embraced the joy of being able to feel.

As the months passed I started to experience a sense of pronounced dissatisfaction. Clients were few and I felt stifled and blocked. I knew

I was good at what I did and the feedback I received was glowing, yet clients were not knocking my door down.

One day, a strange thing happened. A woman I'd never seen before came for an appointment. Halfway through the massage she suddenly spoke, saying she had a message for me from the spirit world. My first reaction was cynical and judgemental. She was a New Age nut who had a barrage of 'guides' floating around passing on indiscriminate titbits. But what came out of her mouth shocked me, especially given its relevant timing. She said I was unable to progress any further because I had more that needed to be forgiven.

This message had been hinted at before, but I'd pushed the hints aside. I didn't want to unearth any more painful memories. I'd had enough hurt and suffering, nearly lost my sanity, not to mention my life. I would be damned if I was going to rake through any more of my history. What more could there possibly be? I just wanted to settle into some kind of peace, find a place for myself where I could finally have a normal existence.

My mind wandered back five years to the last day of the Family of Origin Intensive. We were being led through a meditation to close the door on our past. It was time to say goodbye and let it go. Listening to the voice of the workshop leader, I followed her instruction and visualised myself as a child, pushing with all my might on a very large, solid-wood door. Behind the door was my history, behind me was my guardian angel, watching my attempt to close it. At the time, I wondered why she wasn't helping.

The door closed to within a few inches from the doorframe. I pushed and pushed, but it just wouldn't budge those last few inches. Suddenly, a flash recognition that something remained hidden behind the door, promptly frightened me into pretending I hadn't perceived it. As far as I was concerned I'd done enough.

But it had been as real then as it was now. Everything I tried to initiate in building a new life ultimately hit a dead end. I was being prevented from continuing any further because I had unfinished business that was getting in the way of my progression. Pigheadedly I'd continued to try and forge ahead, wanting to avoid any more revelations, but all I was doing was going around in circles and getting nowhere fast. I also knew that massage was only a means to an end, not my final destination. It had a purpose outside the one I'd assigned to it. Life had its own agenda.

Not only was I trying to avoid further revelations about my history, but also taking seriously flashes of insight I'd received regarding my purpose. They'd started to come during the Family of Origin seminar, and again while I was involved with Suzie. They drove me crazy because I thought I was having delusions. I couldn't understand how it could happen, let alone how I, of all people, could ever be worthy of speaking about spiritual matters.

I figured if I stayed hidden I could avoid it all. I would be safe from exposure and having to face any further risk or fear of failure. But so many things continually went wrong. The more I was stonewalled the more I fought to postpone dealing with either issue. Not knowing if I was deceiving myself with dreams meant for a better person than I, was terrifying. But it was a fight Life was never going to allow me to win. Ultimately, I was forced into confronting what needed to be faced. It was the only way through the deadlock.

I gave in to an urge to write a foundations course for women with a holistic approach to personal and spiritual development. I called it, 'Women's Spiritual Health', designed to run over an eight-week period. Giving myself permission to create it was a hesitant first step toward overriding my mental beliefs that I had nothing worthwhile to offer anyone. The good thing was nobody knew I was writing it. I was safe from any criticism.

What I found most surprising was how easy it was to write. I reconnected with a soulful, creative part of myself I'd left behind long ago. I wanted to ask someone if what I was writing was any good, but my father's voice of mocking contempt punctured my courage and labelled it as rubbish. For months I kept the course in my desk drawer, grappling with what I thought was my audacity to write it.

The idea persisted. I advertised in a local paper seeking expressions of interest. The advert had a reasonable response, so I organised a venue and start date, printed flyers and sent out letters to those who'd contacted me. I intended the group to be small, no more than ten people, and ended up with definite bookings for six. But anxiety over my worthiness to be running such a course plagued me with doubt about my suitability.

Two days before the course was due to begin, the man I'd hired the venue from unexpectedly cancelled its availability. Relieved, I took the opportunity to call it off altogether. I was scared out of my wits.

Disgusted, I threw the course back in my drawer, and over the following months I tried to develop a little more nerve and faith in myself. With bolstered daring, I took the program to the women's centre and presented it as something I passionately believed was missing from the mainstream area of women's health. I knew the coordinator well from my time at the centre and had talked with her then about my interest in developing such a course. She received it kindly, saying she would look at it and get back to me.

When the response came I was politely told it was a good course and well written. However, as it was spiritually based she didn't think a Health Department funded community centre dealing with women in crisis was the right place for it, besides which, I wasn't formally qualified. She had to say no. I took the material home, threw it back in my desk drawer, and went back to massage.

Chapter 11

THE DANCE OF ILLUSION

Nobody is ever allowed to bury themselves unchallenged. Life gives constant feedback and opportunity to correct, heal and grow when our perception of ourselves and life are skewed, regardless of whether we are willing or able to see it. I was blind and in great need, but my beliefs about what I needed, were mistaken.

I had well and truly fallen back into thinking I was alone, the sole power and force in my life. I lived a fear-based and diminished existence because of it, for the simple reason I believed myself to be completely incapable of achieving anything on my own. I needed someone to be the other half of me, to pick up the slack from where I left off in being a whole and capable person. Truly, I hungered to be loved.

But love was as much the elusive mystery it had always been. I was still asking people what it felt like. The only thing I had to go on was my desire for it, an un-nameable longing to be enfolded by it. And I thought it could only be found in the arms of a man. The right man.

I began to imagine the kind of man I'd like to be in partnership with, going so far as to write down his qualities in the form of a letter, asking God and the universe to bring him to me. I was mindful I needed to be very clear about what it was I wanted, stating everything in positive terms, and placing great emphasis on having our relationship be a platform for our mutual growth and healing. I was equally clear I had to be all the other person needed me to be too, otherwise I was being selfish and one-sided. I wanted to cover all my bases with the universe so my request was seen as worthy and sincere.

The letter finished, I folded it up, put it in an envelope and tucked it inside my Bible. I put the Bible back on the bookshelf and let the matter go. God and the universe couldn't deliver my need if I clutched on to it.

In the meantime, I enrolled in a reflexology course. I needed to increase my skills so I would have more to offer clients. On its own, massage wasn't enough anymore. When it was completed, I enrolled in the follow-on Anatomy and Physiology class to take my qualification to the next level.

Struggling with low self-esteem and depression, my daughter moved back in with me not long before her sixteenth birthday. She couldn't cope with the isolation and loneliness of living with her father in the hills any longer. By this time, she'd taken herself off her ADD medication, hating the way it made her feel. Still attending high school, she asked if I would connect my computer to the internet so she could use it for her studies, but I knew it was as much for her desire to stay in contact with her online friends. They'd become her only source of much needed connection and companionship.

I took my time to come around. I had a negative view of my daughter chatting online, and worried about her becoming too involved in a world that wasn't real. She needed flesh and blood people, actual friends her own age she could enjoy being with. In the end I conceded. I didn't want her to be upset with me, but as a mother, I also didn't know how to give her what she so desperately needed.

In her turn my daughter encouraged me to go online and experience it for myself, hoping I'd see it wasn't as bad as I believed. Once set up and shown what to do, I became obsessed. Lonely and isolated myself, chatting provided me with something to fill my own emptiness. I didn't much care to talk to women. I wouldn't admit it, but I'd begun searching for a knight in shining armour, sieving contacts through a veil of mistrust and suspicion.

Finally, I did come across a man who seemed genuine and decent. The only thing I didn't like was that he was a smoker. I hated the smell of cigarettes and the destructiveness of the habit, especially after having watched my father battle throat cancer. In my younger days I'd also been a smoker, but gave it up the moment I discovered I was pregnant with my first child. It really wasn't something I wanted back in my life.

Still, there was no one else and the fact he smoked didn't mean he was a bad person. We chatted on and off for a couple of months before I set about steering us towards a meeting, innocently putting forward a suggestion that next time he came to the city, I'd be happy to cook him dinner. I wanted to meet him and hoped we could be real-life friends.

As our conversations continued, I cautiously looked for any sign he wasn't who he represented himself to be, but none came, apart from the fleeting thought that maybe he drank. His typing was often full of silly spelling mistakes, especially at night. When asked about it, he passed them off as simply being typos because he typed so fast.

Our first planned meeting didn't happen. We both got cold feet. When it came to the crunch it seemed a risk to meet a perfect stranger in my home, and he also had concerns about me. Nevertheless, we were eager to give it another go. Each of us had been living the life of virtual hermits, he in his cabin in the bush, and I in my house in the suburbs. We planned a lunch at a Chinese restaurant instead.

I knew I should say thanks, but no thanks, on our first date. Vince looked considerably knocked about compared to the photo he'd sent me, and his teeth were badly stained with nicotine. He was fidgety and talked about himself a lot, laying his cards on the table. He was unemployed, had baggage with an ex-wife and two children he wasn't allowed to see, and had a long history of things going wrong. He was looking for a woman to bring into his life but didn't have much materially to offer, only himself and all the love in the world for the right lady. He knew exactly the type of person he was looking for and was determined to not settle for less.

Our date over, we headed out to our respective cars. I wondered how I was going to deal with the awkwardness of getting out of making any further plans, when Vince asked if I would sit with him in his car to chat a little longer, he wasn't in a hurry to say goodbye. I couldn't see the harm in a few more minutes of conversation, so obliged.

The time came for me to head off. I had to pick my children up from school. Wanting to make my departure sound friendly but noncommittal, I thanked Vince for lunch and said it had been nice to meet him, now I could put a face to the name. As I went to open his car door to leave, he asked for a kiss, just one little kiss to end the afternoon.

I turned toward him and lifted my face, intending our lips to only brush against each other briefly, but the moment our skin touched an unexpected pleasure shot through me. His lips were like silk and we kissed passionately. Baffled, I said yes when he asked if he could see me again.

The following weekend my sons were at their father's. I invited Vince to my home for dinner, with the clear understanding he would be sleeping on the lounge. I didn't want anything to happen between us other than friendship. My intention was to be cautious and remain in control. I had a vision about what it was I wanted too, and I wasn't going to settle for less either.

Vince arrived right on time, intoxicated and with a cheap cask of wine tucked under his arm. Something about him looked and felt unnervingly familiar. Disappointed, I wanted to send him away, but he'd just driven three hours to be with me. I couldn't turn him around and make him drive all that way back home, especially in the condition he was in.

Right there, in that moment, I felt my shoulders slump. From somewhere deep inside rose the haunting reflection that I didn't deserve any better. No matter how hard I'd tried to walk away from my history, I hadn't succeeded. Here it was again, standing in my doorway. Accepting I was stuck with him, I shoved my uncomfortable feelings aside, lifted my shoulders back, put on a happy face and ushered Vince inside.

My resolve to not have sex that weekend had no backbone. Starved for physical contact and intimacy, I abandoned my strait-laced notions as I relaxed with the wine and played the actress of old, revelling instead in the distraction of the game. It was better than spending yet another friendless Saturday night alone. Besides, it couldn't do any harm. No one need know and after the night was over, I could forget it ever happened.

However, sex and alcohol became an instant and powerful connection between us, though the sex wasn't enjoyable so much in the physical sense. I linked with Vince in a manner I didn't understand, with a thirst that came from a whole other place. His skin, the feel of his body, was enslaving and strangely familiar. I couldn't see as clearly anymore the things I'd seen in the beginning.

The following weekend Vince stayed for two days. One of the first things I did was have him scrub the nicotine stains off his teeth and insist he brush regularly. It astonished me he didn't seem to notice how bad he looked. Cleaning him up and making him appear more presentable, somehow made it easier for me to pretend he was okay.

Before I knew it, Vince was well and truly ensconced in my life, spending more time with me rather than at his own place. When he wasn't with me, I was inundated by phone calls telling me how much he hated being away from me and how much he needed me. I was the woman he'd been looking for all his life. In an unexpected e-mail decorated with images of hearts and flickering candles, he professed his love, sending me into an angry and disappointed tirade.

I'd wanted a man in my life, but I'd wanted to experience romance, the slow calm dance of two people getting to know each other in a meaningful way, before jumping into sex and hurried declarations of love, especially via the internet. Yet here I was, thirsty for touch and having sex like a rabbit with a man who was anything but sober and stabilising.

Feeling invaded and overrun, I tried to hold Vince off, but any attempt on my part at keeping the brakes on our instant relationship were drenched. Vince was like rain falling on a desert. He was lavish with his affection and insistent with his need. I'd become the centre of his universe, and ultimately, he made me feel less alone.

Unable to deflect Vince's earnest and emotional pleas, I caved on my own wishes and agreed to continue seeing him, but with conditions. He had to give up smoking, pull himself together and get a job. It was his only option if he wanted to be with me. Vince agreed readily, saying he understood my position and reassuring me he could be the man I needed him to be. With the deal brokered, I told myself all I needed to do was keep a watchful eye.

Whenever Vince came to stay he always brought with him a ready supply of alcohol. It was an integral part of our play and courtship. Once the clock started ticking towards late afternoon, he'd poor us both a drink. Every day was a party for Vince. I rationalised he was your typical, rough round the edges, country type, who given his situation, had nothing better to do with his time. His way was good-humoured, happy-go-lucky and mischievous.

Good times rolled and I slid into a haze of indulgence, even letting go of my stance on no smoking. Vince said giving up cold turkey was too hard after having been a heavy smoker for too many years. The best he could do was cut down. In its place, I started having the odd cigarette or two, slowly letting it creep back into my own behaviour.

Dinner was being cooked later and later on school nights and what little sense of order I had, disappeared. Vince and I were like wanton teenagers, kissing and canoodling at every opportunity. Our relationship was very heated, day and night. We couldn't get enough of each other. Before long I was leaving my Anatomy and Physiology classes early, making excuses for my departure so I could race back home to be with him when he was in town. He'd become all I could think about.

Vince was a very physical man and an ardent lover. He adored my body and bought me a gold chain with a gold heart that sat just between my breasts. Putting it around my neck, he told me to never take it off. It was his heart I wore close to mine.

Vince took to shuffling my sons away from me whenever they came seeking my companionship and attention. He wanted me all to himself. The watching part of me noticed and I made excuses, allowing my hunger for the prize of someone's time and attention to take priority. I told myself I knew what I was doing, and once things settled and we were more established, he'd be better inclined to share me with my children.

But something nagged and pulled at me, refusing to let me go. Feeling considerably off balance, I literally had to shake my head to clear the fog so I could remember my responsibilities. Taking Vince aside, I tactfully told him the party couldn't go on forever. I needed to re-focus on my family.

Vince's response was to seize the kitchen. He took over cooking the evening meals so they were ready early, and started making helpful suggestions on how I could create a schedule and be more organised. His ideas always came in the afternoons when we were lying on my bed, cuddling and talking about future plans and desires, part of which was living together at some stage. I would listen with a smile but feel the resistance to his suggestions even though they sounded sensible, guarding against giving him a place of power or credibility. My unsureness of him, a feeling that seemed forbiddingly recognisable yet somehow far away, was scrambled up with my fears about trusting any man.

The longer Vince and I were together, the more I noticed his skin had a dull, yellow, bronzy colour. Suddenly it hit me I was having unprotected sex with a man I really didn't know, and I reeled at the possible repercussions. To ease my concerns, Vince agreed to go to a doctor for a thorough health check. A barrage of blood tests were taken and when the results came back, they were clear except for dangerously high cholesterol levels, abnormal iron levels and serious inflammation of the liver.

Automatically, I linked those results to alcohol abuse. But Vince was quick to explain contaminated meat products had been responsible for the damage to his liver years earlier, while working at a meat factory in the country. Seriously ill, it had cost him six months in hospital and during that time he never took a drink, proof he didn't have a problem with alcohol he couldn't control. He was more frightened by his cholesterol levels and put the focus onto changing his diet.

Even so, I carefully chose what I thought were the right words to bring up my concerns about the constant presence of alcohol. I told Vince if he and I were going to be together in the way we'd talked about, it was something that would have to change. I didn't want alcohol in my or my children's life to the degree he drank it. I shared with him that my father had been an alcoholic and the experiences of my childhood had left their mark. He agreed he did drink too much, but really, it was only because he had no reason not to.

Whenever I made a fuss, Vince would smooch and cuddle, pacify and woo me with promises of modifying his drinking as soon as he felt less stressed and more relaxed. He'd tell me to loosen up because I wasn't helping by being so prudish and uptight. I figured maybe he was right. I had to learn to let go and not be so judgemental. My fears were biased, and that wasn't fair on him.

Vince had already laid all his hard luck stories at my feet. I'd heard how he'd lost everything after being retrenched ten years earlier from an executive position in the computer industry, how he'd lost his wife, his home and children immediately after, because she'd only been in the marriage for his wallet. He'd been hit by a falling tree which had almost crushed his skull, and later, what little left to him after his divorce, his treasured mementos of past successes, personal jewellery and photographs, had all been destroyed in a house fire. He had nothing but the clothes on his back and the few odd, second-hand bits and pieces given to him, to furnish his shack.

To top it off, Vince had had a similar background to mine. His own father had been an alcoholic, and he was still entangled in long running issues with his parents and the scars of his childhood. A good deal from his family background struck a chord with my own history, and it scared the hell out of me.

On many levels I could see what was happening, but I was too scattered to act in a unified way, with all parts of myself present and integrated. There was still a huge part of me missing. I battled with the fact the man I was seeing carried many elements from my past.

Adding to the mix, I received a surprise telephone call from the coordinator of the women's centre I'd been involved with earlier. She wanted to know if I still had my Women's Spiritual Health course available. A facilitator running another course on self-esteem and confidence building at the centre had had to pull out. Left with a timetable gap and ten women already signed up, she asked if I'd be interested in running my course in its place. Astonished and excited, I said yes. When our conversation was over, I offered an earnest prayer of thanks to the powers that be. I knew unquestioningly the door had been opened for me.

A few days later I went into the centre for a meeting with the coordinator and asked why she'd thought of me, after all, almost a year had passed since I'd initially approached her, only to be graciously told no. She explained an advertising flyer, printed when I'd first attempted to run my course on my own, found its way onto her desk with a recipe someone had left for her written on the back. Seeing it jolted her memory and presented a solution to the gap in her programming.

Excited and inspired, I re-focused my almost forgotten aspirations and organised the material. This was another new beginning, one that offered to lift me up and move me forward. What I failed to see, was that it was not just a blessed opportunity, but also a well-timed test.

On sunny mornings Vince and I went on drives. He wanted to reminisce and show me the home he once lived in with his ex-wife and children. We'd drive around back roads that skirted the area, inevitably winding up at small taverns or drive through bottle shops. Vince seemed to know where they all were. He'd buy a couple of bottles of beer for himself and a stubby or two of Midori for me. His manner was so blasé it appeared almost natural to be drinking so early, no different from grabbing a coffee or a bottle of water to quench a thirst.

Alarmed, I'd awkwardly decline, making excuses for why I didn't want to drink. Instead, I would subtly try to use my body and my capacity for giving love, to divert Vince's attention away from alcohol, inferring we find a back road or forest path where we could park and make out, but he never took the hints. His only interest was in drinking and nostalgia.

In the evenings, we sat at my little outdoor setting on my front veranda. Topped up from the night before with ample more red wine, Vince would go over and over his painful recollections, all his hurt, anger and bitterness, giving them to me to hold. I tried to use what I'd learnt in the past about boundaries to protect myself from getting swallowed, but it was like struggling to pull myself out of quicksand.

In my effort to hand back Vince's problems and keep the responsibility with him, I encouraged him to seek professional counselling, giving him contact phone numbers of places he could go to get the right sort of help. But he didn't want advice or logical rhetoric, he wanted me to take his pain and make a place for it in my life.

Each time Vince's outpourings hit my resistance, he became sullen and angry. Inside he carried an undiscovered, wounded and angry little boy. I could see him clearly, recognised by the wounded child I still carried inside myself.

There was so much broken in Vince's world, so much pain, and he was crippled by it. He had nightmares that terrified him, and sometimes when we made love, it was as though he tried to get all the way inside me, so he could hide and be safe. The healer in me tried to salve his wounds, but I just got drawn in deeper.

My home life inevitably turned into a muddled shamble. My children's behaviour became considerably unrulier as they were pushed further into the background. There was no structure, no order left whatsoever. Unable to hold the reigns I seemed to disintegrate. The weight of Vince's issues and painful emotions, the alcohol and rising tension, his expectation that I had room for it all in my home, in my life, turned me to pulp.

Seeing I was losing my grip, Vince insisted on taking me to his place in the country on my childfree weekends. He wanted to get me away from the demands of motherhood and give us a chance to have some uninterrupted alone time. He loved to cook for me and show me around his territory, adamant I relax and let go of all my troubles. Vince liked nothing more than to see me dressed only in one of his tee-shirts, loosening up with a drink in my hand.

On my first visit, I saw the huge piles of empty wine casks and beer can boxes stacked behind the kitchen door. I saw the dirt and smelt the stench of something unholy. I saw the way he lived, the dirty bed linen, the cigarette ash all over everything and the dirty glasses scattered on his computer desk, sticky with the remnants of stale red wine.

That was where Vince spent his time at home, chatting on the internet, living through a dream world of software and stupefying addiction. I saw it all and pretended I didn't. I ignored the truth of my eyes and the tightening of my gut. I didn't value myself enough to act on my feelings of repulsion, and I didn't value myself enough to not be willing to breathe in the smell of his bed. I just set about cleaning up.

I washed all his jumpers and bedding to get the cigarette smoke and smell out of them, and helped sort out his clothes. We took all the rubbish to the tip and I cleaned his house. I figured all diamonds come out of the ground and Vince was a diamond just waiting to be dug up. All I had to do was brush off the dirt and let a little light into his world.

Swept up in scenarios of Vince's future redemption, I told myself it was all fixable. There was nothing the power of love couldn't conquer if two people were prepared to work at it. I imagined the kind of successful, competent man he must have been before his downfall. He was there, buried underneath all the pain and suffering. If we could heal that, the man underneath the addiction would be mine.

I began to delicately point out to Vince the many stops he made for alcohol whenever we were on the road, impressing on him he lived a very unhealthy lifestyle, and restating it was not the way I wanted to live. Gradually he came around to acknowledging he did have a drinking problem, and we talked about a time when he would go into detox. When he was ready, I would be his support person.

In the meantime, the start date to the women's group loomed close, and I spiralled into self-doubt. Something wasn't right. Up until two days prior to the course commencing, I tried to think of excuses I could use to get out of it. The only thing that got me through was staying mindful of the opportune events that opened the door at the centre in the first place. God must have thought I was ready, and if God thought I was ready, I had to trust that faith in me, even if I didn't have faith in myself.

The first day arrived, and as the women and I sat in a circle on the floor, the energy and presence that is always available when people come together to heal, was palpable in the room. It settled over everyone. As each woman gave her name and told a little of her story, I marvelled at how 'God/Life' works. I knew their stories intimately. Filled with renewed confidence I could bring something soothing and healing to their lives, I felt a deep sense of wonder and gratitude for the privilege.

As the course got underway, I was also busy encouraging Vince to leave the unemployment of the bush for better prospects in the city. It seemed a logical step. Once he was back in the workforce his self-esteem would improve, and he would have better access to counselling services to help with his drinking. I had all the answers, knew all the right steps to take, and after some initial unease on Vince's part about change, he was keen and happily optimistic. It was decided he would stay with me for a week or two while he looked for a place to live.

It wasn't long before Vince found accommodation, and the day he officially moved to Perth, was the day I realised I may have underestimated what I was dealing with. He was so drunk I couldn't understand how he hadn't smashed himself into a tree or oncoming traffic while towing his trailer full of belongings over such a tediously long distance. That day we had our first, real, heated augment, and I had my first undeniable glimpse of an old and menacing shadow.

I hadn't noticed until that moment how much Vince's temperament and facial expressions were like my father's. They had many of the same mannerisms and were of a similar build and height. I wanted Vince out of my life right then and there, but I couldn't just dump him. It was because of me he was here. I had to follow through on what I'd started, at least until he got back on his feet.

Vince told me our fight was my fault. As far as he was concerned he had every right to drink given he was so strained over the conditions of his life. He'd made a big move and it was all for me, therefore I had to back off and behave like a proper woman. From then on, I was caught in a spiralling tailspin. The impact of what I was involved in set in as sheer panic, but I was in no way able to pull myself out of it. I'd already stayed too long and succumbed to a trance from long ago.

Established in his new environment, Vince quickly settled into the same lifestyle he'd lived in the country, and I was confronted more visibly with the severity of his habits. The three most vital things in Vince's existence were alcohol, cigarettes, and his chat rooms on the internet. I soon learned I didn't even come close to rating fourth. He was drinking all the time, getting drunker than I'd ever seen him, and becoming generally disgruntled about everything.

Friction intensified between us as I began to express my alarm and uneasiness with his activities, and my dislike of the way he was increasingly attempting to separate me from my sons, particularly when we were all together at his house. My boys were persistently being told to go and play, and I was being told I had to let them go so they could grow up. Mostly they weren't allowed inside but had to remain outside to play. Vince said he didn't think the man he was boarding with would appreciate his home being invaded by children, and he didn't want to do anything that would put his landlord offside. Vince's allegiance was to whoever was providing him sanctuary.

As was Vince's way, he took over as social organiser in his new surroundings. It was summer so backyard barbeques by the swimming pool became the order of the day. His landlord didn't seem to mind at all. In fact, he appeared delighted to have the company. But I walked a precarious line. Vince became angry over any sign from me I was watching out protectively for my children. His thinly disguised intolerance of my sons inevitably ended our gatherings in embarrassing outbursts that left me reeling.

At a loss to understand what had happened to our loving relationship, and all the promises made, I found myself performing the dance of pacification, appeasing my children and trying to keep them safe, all the while endeavouring to avoid Vince's dissatisfaction, but it was a dance I could never get right.

Strangely, I had an unexpected dream with a very clear message. In the dream a higher part of myself was counselling me to let Vince go. It told me that in order to have a healthy, functional relationship, both parties had to be whole and present within themselves. During the dream I was conscious of what was happening and knew it was spiritual guidance. In the morning when I woke, I pretended it was just a silly dream, not a message I should take heed of. I knew I was flying in the face of what was best for me, but I couldn't let him go. I just tried harder to make things work.

Coincidentally, in my Anatomy and Physiology classes, we'd begun covering the impact alcohol and other drugs had on the body, particularly in heavy users over sustained periods of time. The topic was graphic and frightening. Upset, I abruptly cut class one afternoon and drove straight to Vince's house, intending to break up with him. I didn't want the kind of life I feared was in store for me and my children if I stayed with him. But leaving wasn't going to be the cut and dried ending I'd wanted.

Vince was furious. How typical he said. I move him from his home, which took the last of his savings to pay for, and here I was running like a coward because things were getting a little tough. He reminded me if it hadn't been for his mother standing firm, his father would never have been able to recover from his alcoholism. The implication was if I gave up on him, he'd be lost, and it would be because of my weakness, not his.

I began a mental war with myself, trying to understand if I was judging Vince harshly, or if I rightly didn't have to have his sickness in my life. I'd been clear on the way over to his house I needed to end the relationship, but Vince's ensuing reproach turned my resolve to dust.

Vince was my responsibility. I'd uprooted him and filled his head full of ideas about a new life. He moved for me. He was willing to undergo the trials of getting sober, for me, and I was backing out and letting him down at the first bump in the road. I was a selfish and self-preserving coward. Like a scolded child I apologised for being so untrustworthy and hard-hearted, and reaffirmed my commitment to stick by him.

Convinced I was the one in the wrong, I put myself back on dexamphetamine, taking them from my son's prescription. If I could get myself thinking right, be positive, happy and upbeat, I'd be more like what Vince wanted. He would love me again and be motivated to follow through on his promises of getting straight. I'd be someone worth doing it for. I pulled out of my Anatomy and Physiology class altogether.

I couldn't remember the seriousness of what it meant to be with an alcoholic. I couldn't even bring myself to use the word out loud. I couldn't remember the life my mother had lived, and I couldn't remember what it had meant to me as a child, until things started happening to remind me.

Vince was playing with one of my boys in the kitchen one evening. I was smiling but watching nervously from where I stood cooking dinner. Vince and one of my sons were laughing; right up until Vince miscalculated the distance between my son's face and the floor as he turned him over in a summersault.

The laughing turned to howling and the scene before me began to warp and displace, as if I were witnessing a glitch in time. I flashed back to the kitchen of my childhood and thought I saw Vince and my father standing in each other's bodies. It shook me to the core.

As I rushed to comfort my son, Vince noticed the concerned look of horror on my face, and reacted with defensive anger. He said his ex-wife used to look at him like that, and had always interfered between him and his sons when they'd played. Shocked, I placated my son and smoothed things over with Vince so he wouldn't get angrier.

A couple of weeks later we were all spending the night at Vince's. His landlord was away for the weekend. After dinner and a bath, I set about readying the boys for lights out. Vince was in a good mood and had begun playing with my other son. Unexpectedly, he jokingly picked him up and threw him into his bed, misjudging the force he used to throw him. When my son's back hit the headboard with a heavy thud, his bewildered and frightened eyes looked for mine. I felt sick inside.

At the ensuing eruption of anxious crying, Vince's head whipped around to look for the expression on my face, already on the attack with his defence. I stood transfixed in the bedroom doorway with my heart thumping, feeling startled and dazed. I wanted to grab my boys and get the hell out of there. But I couldn't move. My legs felt heavy and rooted to the floor, caught by a paralysis I couldn't fathom.

Worried and worn, I confronted Vince more forcibly with my fears and concerns, adding further fuel to his fire. He said I made him out to be a lush and he didn't see himself that way, or as a danger to anyone. I wasn't being very comforting, he said, and it was my job to make him feel comfortable.

Vince became irate at my persistence in making alcohol, and my children's wellbeing, an issue. His spitefulness pinched on his face, he erupted, telling me in no uncertain terms he didn't see why he should have to care about my sons, when he wasn't able to be a father to his own.

Powerless to deny anymore the unacceptable position my children and I were in; I pushed the matter of counselling, telling Vince his baggage over his children, and his alcohol abuse, were not things I could put up with any longer. He had to follow through on his promises to get straight, or it was over between us.

Separately, we finally went into counselling with an organisation that worked specifically with substance abuse and addiction. But Vince only attended two sessions. Although I was disappointed, I was in so deep I defended him to my counsellor when she tried to show me a picture of reality. I preferred to think she had no empathy and was spiritually deficient in her judgement and attitude. I was also getting agitated in general with being back in this type of counselling. I didn't want to hear it.

I continued for a few more sessions, and tried to implement boundaries about alcohol in my home at least, excluding it altogether. Vince's solution was to drink his fill and get drunk before coming to my house, gradually bringing one bottle of beer, then two, in brown paper bags, sheepishly sliding them onto my kitchen benchtop.

As our liaison continued we clashed ever more dramatically, yet we persisted in saying we loved each other. A great deal of our fighting was now being done over the internet, via e-mails. I would spend all day constructing the perfect epistle that would say everything needing to be said, always with a slant on fixing and changing Vince's behaviour. I wrote great long letters expressing how I felt and pointing out the things that were wrong. Some were break-up letters I left in his mail box, only to go running back to retrieve them before they were found.

I couldn't figure out what the hell was going on. Why was I so involved with a man who was suffering such soul-destroying problems, and why couldn't I leave? On the one hand, I saw the alcoholic and felt the fear engendered, and on the other saw with compassion all the reasons why he was the way he was. It was what I knew best. But the double-sided view pulled me mercilessly in two.

Vince kept telling me I couldn't see the real man, only the low-life alcoholic. It was the reason why he drank so heavily, declaring he never used to drink as much when it was just him in his little house in the bush. I made him feel bad about himself and I put him under so much additional pressure. Didn't I understand how hard it was for him? Didn't I have any consideration for his pain? Couldn't I just back off and accept him as he was?

I started leaving my boys with my daughter a couple of nights a week so I could sleep over at Vince's house. He demanded I make the effort for him as his partner, but it was also his solution to the alcohol ban in my home. I'd plead with my daughter to do it for me, and manipulate her with guilt so she would cooperate when she didn't want, or couldn't cope with the responsibility. All I could think about was myself and not alienating Vince any further.

The nights were never a pleasant experience. Vince would cook our meal and keep the wine flowing, making sure both our glasses were always full, especially his. I started refusing to drink beyond a glass or two. The less I drank, the more revolting he became. We'd sit at the kitchen table and smoke multitudes of cigarettes while watching TV or arguing, until it was time for bed.

In bed I would submit my body to be used, while in my mind I'd think how familiar this was to something hidden in the dark. The love had well and truly gone out of it and sex played out porno movie style. I'd be numb and obliging to what he required as he positioned my body where he wanted it, his tongue devouring my face. After it was over, and Vince lay snoring next to me, I lay unmoving and awake beside him, desperately wanting to get up and go home, never to return. But I couldn't move. Something unfathomable always kept me pinned to the bed.

Vince's behaviour had become terribly dark, depressive and abusive. He started coming to my home at night, drunk and sullen, monopolising me and my time. Ushered outside to the back patio, he'd go over more from his history, what he wanted from me, what I wasn't delivering, and hitting out verbally with a great deal of judgmental criticism about the imperfections of my children.

Dreams of my father began to plague my sleep. I found myself sitting in front of him trying to speak words of long-ago suffering, but when I opened my mouth, nothing would come out. Dropping my shoulders in grief and defeat, I'd give up trying. In each one of my dreams my father simply got up and walked away, leaving me sitting in hopeless, wretched tears. I'd wake up choking on the words still stuck in my throat. Most disturbingly, I had no idea what the words were.

I knew there were similarities between these two men that were acting as the prompt. I came to realise I'd drawn Vince in because it was time to deal with the remainder of my worries from my history. There was something I hadn't learnt yet, only I couldn't figure out what it was.

There was of course, still the possibility Vince and I were meant to be together. I had never experienced this kind of intense connection with a man. Before things had turned so ugly I'd even seen aura colours of a deep crimson during love-making. Surely it had to be the real thing. We were spiritually linked.

My wise part saw what was happening and understood the unfolding events, yet passed no judgement about what action I should take. My tailspin had turned into a nose dive that was out of control, and there was nothing I could do about it. I'd fallen too close to the ground.

All I could do was acknowledge I was in process, allow the events to play out, and recognise this was happening for a reason. I was determined to work through it until I'd gained everything from it I needed to learn. If I didn't, I'd just bring the lesson in again in another form. Life doesn't allow us to get away with anything.

I frequently remembered the impact of that first telephone call from the women's centre offering me the opportunity to run my course. When it had come, I'd not been with Vince long and was in the initial stages of struggling with the recognition of what I'd drawn into my life. In truth it had been a crossroads moment, one where I'd been given the challenge to stop and look from the pain, suffering, abuse, self-hate and constant battle of the past, to what could be before me in the future.

I'd been presented with a choice over what it was I really wanted. Both situations had presented themselves at almost the same time. I asked myself who it was I really wanted to be, and if I had the courage to be that person, to believe in myself. What most reflected the face of my soul?

I knew what sort of life I wanted. I knew my spiritual path and the work I wanted to do, yet here I was, involved with a man who embodied all that brought heaviness and tears back into my life. The fact that I was still actively running the Women's group made it feel doubly unacceptable.

When I was with the women, I felt inspired and empowered. I was helping others begin the process of assessing for themselves the quality of their lives and the degree to which they were living authentically, yet outside of that role, my life was a mess. I was too ashamed to tell anyone I'd become slave to my own unresolved, addictive patterns. I couldn't even admit it to myself. I began to show up unprepared, tired and distracted as the clash between my two worlds magnified. Yet by the end of the term, it was clear the group had been a resounding success. The Centre's coordinator was pleased with the outcome and wanted to offer it as a regular part of each terms' programming. No one could have been more elated than I.

But I was in a hopeless situation. I ceased to focus on my work and my own life altogether. I turned to Tarot cards again, obsessively doing readings long into the night, frantically trying to find guidance and to comprehend the incomprehensible. All they did was add to my confusion, spinning my mind with double-sided imagery and metaphors. What was I missing? What was I not getting right? If I could just get it right everything would be ok.

My relationship had become a spiritual quandary. It had come down to trying to understand right from wrong, what was 'spiritually correct' as opposed to 'spiritually incorrect' in judging Vince. Could I walk away and let him go to his own fate without being judged by God in turn for being a selfish and unloving person? Or could I be selfish and put myself and my own wellbeing and happiness first, without it hanging over me as a crime.

In the final analysis, my mental warring and inability to be the leader in my own life, determined my behaviour. I was looking to know the mind of God, so I couldn't possibly make any more damning mistakes.

Chapter 12

CONNECTING THE DOTS

VINCE saw I was not the woman I had been when we first met. Bit by bit I'd let go of my power, gaining me nothing but scorn - his and mine. He said I had potential, talent and possibilities in life. It made him angry I wasn't out there using my talents to my advantage. Here he was, all washed up with no prospects and no future, watching me waste mine. He reminded me I had to be the main breadwinner so we could afford to live together. All he had to contribute was his love, support and sexual prowess.

Vince decided the solution to our situation was for me to buy a bigger home with an area for he and I, separate from where my boys would be. Once in a stable environment he felt sure he'd be able to control his drinking. I was terrified at the idea. It would be a living hell.

Despite my horror, I organised to have my home appraised and put on the market. Vince came with me to look at a couple of other houses the following day, and I was embarrassed to be with him. Still slightly drunk from the night before, he took over in telling the real estate agent what I wanted and how I wanted it. Panicked, I came to my senses and took my house off the market three days later.

Even though I continued to be involved with Vince, I refused to be an avenue through which he could hide anymore. I became a harsh mirror that never let up, and he hated that I could see through him. When it came right down to it, he had no intention of not drinking. The very idea was terrifying to him beyond anything I could understand.

Vince just wanted to be accepted as he was, without having to change a thing, while I struggled to separate the past from the present, and reality from fantasy.

Unable to manage anymore, or let him go, I went back into counselling. I felt myself getting closer to dealing with the truth, whatever it was, but it was a tentative step.

At my first session it was obvious my new counsellor was someone who was going to be important to me. I could feel the guidance my life has always had when I've been willing to listen.

After blurting out my situation, one of the first things he asked was if I'd heard of John Bradshaw. I took great delight in telling him I had, in fact I had many of his books. I related to, and appreciated his work, and yes, I had a copy of *Home Coming, Reclaiming and Championing Your Inner Child*. I'd had it for years but never managed to read it through. For some reason it made me angry. Rather than throw it out, I left it on the shelf, feeling a day might arrive when I would be ready. I guessed that day had come.

My counsellor's request was that I go home and read the book, if not read it, thumb through its pages until I found something relevant. I could feel my opposition to the suggestion, the immediate presence of anger, so knew I had to do it.

That night I sat with the book in my hands. I began to laugh as I read a few lines of the first chapter. This was stupid, I told myself. I don't need to read this damn book. Angrily I slammed it shut. I could feel the rage begin to surge. I opened the book again, but this time, I did it with my eyes closed, asking for guidance to the message it had for me. I knew I still wasn't going to be able to read the whole thing through.

I found myself looking at chapter eleven, *Protecting Your Wounded Inner Child*, and felt the first sting of tears. I knew I was not protecting my inner child from the man I was involved with, nor was I protecting my external children. As I turned the page, my eyes dropped to the sub heading, *Communicating with Your Inner Child*. Oh no, I groaned, we're back to that again, the non-dominant handwriting. I'd found what I needed.

I knew something profound was taking place. All I'd been through in the past taught me to trust the process, to trust the spiritual hand of Life. That night, I deeply surrendered to what I knew was now inevitable.

While my boys were playing in the next room, I sat at the kitchen table and began. Immediately, I connected. What follows are conversational excerpts with my Inner Child from my journal. These are the final missing pieces to the puzzle of my life, beginning Thursday the 21st of March, eleven days after my 43rd birthday, one of the loneliest and most despairing days of my life.

> Thurs. 21st March. 2002:
>
> Hello, what would you like me to call you?
>
> *Sara.*
>
> Why Sara? That's not your name.
>
> *Because I'm hiding. I don't want anyone to know who I am.*
>
> Why is that Sara?
>
> *Because I get in trouble, I have to hide.*
>
> Where are you hiding?
>
> *In the closet.*

(I remembered a bodywork session I'd had several years previous, where the practitioner had used certain types of massage techniques to stimulate trapped energy in my body. I'd attended because I wanted to expose things I knew were still hidden from my awareness. At my first session, I experienced myself as being very small, locked in what felt like the dark space of a closet. The abject feeling of terror associated with it prevented me from penetrating the dark, or recalling anything further, but I had the distinct impression I was only three years old.)

How old are you Sara?

I'm three.

What do you look like Sara?

I don't have a body.

How can you not have a body?

I'm invisible. I can feel you trying to give me another name. If you do I'll get angry and won't talk to you anymore.

(I was thinking of her as me.)

Okay, I won't call you by my name. You can be Sara.

I hate children.

(At this point I was getting quite angry with my boys for being so noisy in the next room.)

Why do you hate children Sara?

Because they are bad, they do bad things.

Do you do bad things Sara?

Yes, that's why I'm invisible so I don't have to see myself.

Why are you talking to me Sara?

Because it's time you found me. I have blonde hair you know, I'm not you.

(I remembered another dream I'd had years before. I was in a dentist's waiting room with all my family, except the youngest sister because she hadn't been born yet. We were looking through photographs of ourselves as children when one of my family members took a picture I was holding from me, asking to have a look at it. When it was handed back, the picture was of a little girl with blonde hair. I didn't recognise her and became very upset, wanting to know who she was. I wanted my proper picture back, but my family insisted it was the same picture. I became terribly frightened.)

Then who are you Sara?

I don't know.

How did you get into the closet? Did someone put you in there?

You did!

At that point, I'd had enough. I felt tired and agitated. The noise from my sons was driving me crazy. They were only playing and laughing but I felt threatened and needed to shut the noise out. Hurriedly I went about getting them to bed, all the while concentrating on not losing control. I had the feeling I was getting close to some kind of discovery, and I was afraid.

Once the boys were taken care of I lay on my bed, putting myself in an open position, breathing deeply to ease the uncomfortable feelings in my chest and release the agitation. It was a practice I'd been doing for a while, and something I trusted. It nearly always worked, often resulting in me getting in touch with sensations in my body. I didn't always understand what they meant, but I never questioned there was a reason for them. I would simply go with the flow, and let my body do what it needed to do. It was enough to know energy was being shifted.

This time, sensations I'd felt previously were magnified. My mouth opened and my face twisted in a much more pronounced and contorted way than ever before. My mouth opened so wide I thought my jaw might split in two. Suddenly, I felt a huge rush of fear, and an upsurge of raw emotion. Quietly I sobbed myself to sleep. The next evening, I began again with my journal.

Fri. 22nd March. 2002

Hello Sara. Would you like to talk to me?

Go away.

What's wrong, why won't you talk to me?

Because you made me do a bad thing.

How did I make you do a bad thing?

I can't say.

Why can't you say Sara, are you afraid?

Yes I'm afraid. I have to stay hidden. Then nothing and no one can see me. I don't exist.

If you don't exist how come I can talk to you?

Because you are in here with me.

How did I get in there?

You have always been in here but you just didn't know it. You have been asleep.

Then how come you say no one can see you. You're hiding from everyone and everything.

Because you have only just become aware of me. You have come to get me out.

How can I have come to get you out if I have been in there with you the whole time?

Because you have just woken up. You have perceived a different awareness.

You sound too old to be three, you sound much older. Why is that?

Because my mind has grown.

Sara, you said I made you do something bad. What was it I made you do?

I don't have the words.

Sara, why did I put you in the closet?

Because you blamed me, you didn't want to remember. I live with it so you don't have to.

Closing the journal, I began to shake. My body felt weak and I became intensely nauseated. It was getting late and I needed to get my boys off to bed. I was not feeling safe, and knew they had to be out of harm's way. Again I got them settled as soon as I could. Once all was quiet, I knew what I had to do.

I lay myself on my bed, feeling emotion rise instantly. I tried to relax and breathe as deeply as I could. In my mind I asked to be shown what it was all about. What was it that the little girl felt so ashamed of, and why had I locked her in the dark? My face began to contort, my mouth slowly opening. I soothed myself with the thought of spirit, with the protection I knew was around me, and fully let myself go.

Suddenly I could feel something in my mouth. Instantly knowing what it was, I began to gag and choke. My jaw felt like it was going to rip apart. The tears came as I struggled to breathe, my eyes bulged and the screams in my head bounced off the walls in my mind. My body stiffened, I became immobilised, too frightened to move. I was fully aware of what was happening, trusting I was safe. All I had to do was go with the process.

At that point, I remembered another dream. I'd woken in an intensely painful state, choking from a bulging python in my throat. The dream had given me the symbols, but I wouldn't believe it because I couldn't consciously remember it. The whole idea was just too disgusting. Surely it could have represented any number of things. It didn't have to be a penis. But I couldn't deny it now.

I felt it in my mouth being thrust in and out, covering my nose and choking me.

Huge waves of grief and disbelief coursed through my body as I rounded into a tight ball, heaving into my pillow. For days following I was spitting up mucus, and experiencing the constant sensation in my mouth.

I was three years old when it happened.

I went straight to my journal.

Sat. 23rd March 2002

Hello Sara, would you like to talk to me?

You know what he did.

Am I right, Sara?

Yes. I couldn't breathe he was choking me. It happened over and over.

Did anything else happen Sara?

No, I have been here and you grew. I am the real Lyn.

Are you telling me I am not Lyn?

Yes.

Then who am I?

You are an empty person. You aren't real without me. You're a shadow without content. My mind has grown through you.

Do you have anything else to tell me Sara?

No. I am in you now.

Who has come home, you or me?

You have.

I have never been able to handle anyone putting their hands around my face or near my nose. Even when playing with my children, or just cuddling and they get too close to my nose, I become instantly panic-stricken, breaking away gasping for my next breath. The feeling has always been one of terror and suffocation. Trying to figure it out, I'd wondered if my uncle had put his hands over my six-year-old face to stifle any noise I might have made, the night he came to my bed. But now I had the right answer.

Throughout the remainder of the day, I could feel Sara's presence inside me. The next morning, I could hear her crying. Using my journal, I checked in to see what was happening.

> Sun. 24th March. 2002
>
> Sara, I can hear you crying, what's wrong?
>
> *I'm so lonely I hurt deep. I have no words just this sound…..Ahhhhhhh*
>
> That's the sound I make sometimes when I cry because the pain is so bad.
>
> *You are expressing me.*
>
> Sara, can you and I heal this together? Or do we need someone else.
>
> *I only need you.*
>
> You need a lot of attention from me don't you.
>
> *Yes.*
>
> I promise I will never leave you again Sara.

Many things were beginning to fall into place. I understood that as a three-year-old, I'd been so traumatised by what had happened I'd split that part of myself off completely, putting the memory and the child, who I'd disguised in disgust, in the darkness of a closet. I'd created a false self and grown up, leaving her behind to live with the memory and the shame.

Later that same day, my boys were being very noisy, laughing and playing rough with each other. I became highly agitated and paced the room. I could feel the rage inside, could feel the way I wanted to hurt them. I grabbed my journal and put myself in my bedroom, closing the door behind me.

> Sara I feel really agitated and angry right now, can you tell me what is happening?
>
> *I hate children.*
>
> Why Sara, why do you hate children?
>
> *Because they are wild and expressive.*

> Why does that bother you?
>
> *Because I want to be and I can't. It brings attention.*
>
> What sort of attention Sara?
>
> *Bad.*
>
> Do you get in trouble?
>
> *I get crushed and squashed.*

Right then I had a huge realisation. All the anger and rage I'd ever felt at my children over the years was Sara's anger and rage. She hated children because they were bad. They did bad things. Playful, innocent behaviour brought unwanted attention, of the nasty kind. It was Sara's experience that childhood had to be compressed and extinguished. In a later talk with Sara, she gave me permission to call her by her real name, Lyn. I had found a lost part of myself.

During this journal writing, my emotional state had grown sad and needy. I cried a lot, and was sometimes inconsolable, wanting only to feel arms around me and as though someone cared, but it couldn't happen. My core beliefs were, I am un-loveable, I do not deserve love and I am all alone. It made perfect sense then, given those beliefs, I drew into my life emotionally unavailable men.

I became more and more upset, lonely and tearful. I had a desperate need to be with my boyfriend, to feel him comfort me and hold me safe. I would ring and ask him to come and be with me, only to be fobbed off with suggestions to go and relax, watch a movie or get an early night. The truth is Vince was always bunkered in with his alcohol and the internet, unable as he was unwilling, to respond. I would become overwhelmed with grief and feelings of rejection, but didn't comprehend why until I bothered to ask the right question. What is this about?

I lay myself down on my lounge and allowed myself to fully go into the grief I felt. Hugging my knees tightly and burying my face, I began to sob such wretched sobbing. The pain was intense. Suddenly I began to call for my mother. I was small, afraid and fragile. I remembered another dream I'd had a long time ago, of myself as a cripple pulling and dragging my body along the ground, begging my mother to come and help me. But she wouldn't come; she just stood at a distance and watched me crawl.

In that moment I realised how the little girl, so starved for care and affection, was trying to get the love and attention she never received as a child. She was trying to resolve her history. All I could do was cry harder at the cruelty of it. The more honest insight I gained, the more the little girl and I grieved.

A couple of days later, I found myself more accepting of my loneliness. I knew I wasn't going to get the comfort I craved. It was impossible because it was something I had to resolve on my own. When the evening came and all was quiet, I decided to watch a video and put my feet up, spending the time with myself in a deliberate effort to not wallow in more self-pity.

I had three videos in my car I hadn't had a chance to watch yet, so went out to retrieve one, grabbing in the dimness the first to touch my hand. It was a movie called *Quills*, which detailed the life of the Marquis De Sade, played by Geoffrey Rush. The Marquis had been judged to be a sexually depraved man because of his beliefs and writings depicting debauchery and sexual torture. He was incarcerated in a Catholic asylum by the State and the Church, convicted of being evil, a work of the devil himself. Kate Winslet played the part of a servant girl who lived and worked at the asylum. She was both mesmerized and repulsed by the Marquis, developing a friendship with him that liberated her curious and stifled imagination.

I had no idea what the movie was about when I sat down to watch it. As the story unfolded, it stunned me into stillness with graphic images portraying sexual abuse and constant dark references to the devil. It embodied much of the torment I'd lived with regarding the Church, God, and the terrifying power of evil. Several times I was so disgusted and angered I wanted to turn it off, but told myself not to be so stupid, it was only a movie.

Truly I was captivated, feeling a close affinity with the servant girl. More and more I was drawn into the story, as though I were a part of it. As the movie came nearer to the end, I could feel my body as tight as a drum, almost in anticipation of what was coming.

The inevitable happened, and the servant girl was brutally raped, tortured and murdered. It was a grotesquely violent ending, one that left me totally shocked and devastated. I had such a close feeling with this servant girl, it was as though it had happened to me.

I began to cry, as I do when movies have such a sad and tragic ending. I acknowledged my sadness and reassured myself it was okay to cry, but the tears turned to sobbing. I shook myself thinking I shouldn't be so upset, except the sobbing continued to intensify. I tried to calm myself, telling myself I'd been triggered by the content of the movie, and it would pass. I got up from the lounge and went out to the kitchen.

The deep sobbing began to wrack my whole body as I crossed over into hysteria. Something was terribly wrong. I paced the floor out of my mind with guttural terror, eyes bulging wide with fear and disbelief. I ran into my room choking back huge inrushes of air as I began to hyperventilate. Sitting myself on the edge of my bed, I rocked back and forth, thoughts wildly racing through my mind. Repetitively, I frantically asked myself what on earth was going on, what was this about?

I felt the presence of the wise part and understood something significant was taking place, and I had to work with it. I allowed myself to go further into what I was feeling, letting it build, and repeating the question out loud, "What is this about?"

My father's presence forced its way through. I pushed him away, telling myself I really had gone over the edge. Words tumbled out of my mouth as I shook my head crying, "No! No! Not my father, it's not true." The rocking grew faster as the wise part in me watched, and as I felt the watching, I let go of my resistance. I had to let it go all the way.

Abruptly a sinister image broke through to the surface. I was ten years old and lying on the polished wood floorboards of a darkened room. The bowels of hell had opened up in the floor beneath me, casting the light of dancing orange and yellow flames across the walls, filling the room with an eerie glow. I'd fallen in, only to be instantly spat out, but when I came out, I'd been dramatically and forever changed.

What sat on the edge of hell was the same ten-year-old, but with eyes glowing like red hot coals, wearing an evil smirk and looking contemptuously at me. She wore the same outfit as the little girl in my vision of the child in white, though now it was all tarnished and wrinkled. With the image came complete comprehension. I knew what had happened. The missing pieces of the puzzle drew together across time, and the dots connected.

My father had attempted to rape me. I do not know if he physically succeeded all the way in his effort. At the time it occurred I disassociated in order to survive the experience. The understanding about what happened and the effect it had on me came symbolically, protecting me from a shock I wouldn't have been able to handle otherwise.

The brutal trauma of the experience caused my psyche to literally split in two. The child in white, my essential, authentic spiritual self, disappeared in a coma as she fell through the hole in the floor, vanishing to some other place. What remained in my body was the image my father gave me of myself as he whispered his slurred, self-justifying, degrading mumblings into my ear while lying on top of me, fumbling with his belt.

As the reality of what I comprehended sunk in, my mind froze. I told myself this couldn't be real. Holding back my breath as if to somehow hold back the revelation, I grabbed my journal and began to frantically write, and as I wrote, the evil voice of long ago returned to laugh victoriously in my head.

> Hello, can I talk to the part of Lyn that remembers what she is feeling terror about?
>
> *What do you want?*
>
> Tell me why I am so afraid. What is wrong? Tell me what happened.

Ha Ha Ha Ha Ha, Evil happened.

What sort of evil?

The bowels of hell opened and she fell in, regurgitated Evil.

Tell me about that, what happened?

You know what happened, he forced himself on you and said you deserved it.

He said you liked it. It was not bad for him to do it because you were already bad.

He was blameless. It was your fault.

You made him do it because you were so innocent and he wanted to crush it.

The devil has lived in you since.

Who was it?

You know who it was.

No, I don't. I need you to tell me.

Yes you do. You're just too afraid to say. He was very drunk. It was dark, not much light. He fumbled and muttered to himself the whole way through. He didn't even care it was you, he just wanted to destroy.

For the next two hours I paced around my house, roving like a mad woman from one room to another. I had to keep moving. To stay still was an unbearable agony. In my mind I spoke soothingly to myself, having a conversation with the pain, trying to keep myself intact. I rocked, cried a river of tears, and let myself grieve the deepest wound of all. I'd finally found the answer to the mystery of why I have felt so evil and relentlessly pursued through life by the devil, battling with my sanity and will to live.

The next day and for days following, I was in shock. I didn't know how I was supposed to feel. What was I supposed to do with the information?

It was like having a scorching ball in my hands, passing it rapidly from one to the other so as not to feel it burn. I felt completely suspended in time, just trying to let the reality fully sink in. I went through thoughts of labelling myself insane, but knew that wasn't true. I'd already tried to hide behind insanity in the past. I'd grown too strong for that now. It was not an option for me any longer.

I slowly became aware of a feeling of relief in amongst the trauma. I had an energy and clarity that was in opposition to the rest of me. As the days passed, subtle feelings of fullness settled inside my chest, and I stopped to smile at it often. It was a strange sensation I had no words for other than, warm, yet intellectually I still struggled with the mind-blowing disclosure.

Over the following week, I moved through the process of integrating the last of my memories. There were moments of despair and desperate neediness. Again, I sought comfort from my boyfriend and again could not find what I longed for. He was unable to be present for me, or respond to my need to be held and comforted. I felt the wall around him wanting to keep me out.

I took my journal to the counsellor I was seeing. Sitting before him still in shock, I fumbled with disjointed sentences trying to tell him everything. Before I had time to finish what I needed to say, he was looking at his watch and saying we had to stop, our session was over. My eyes felt like saucers as I blinked uncomprehendingly, my mouth open mid-sentence. I had only just got to the part about my father.

When I left the building and walked out onto the footpath, I had the same feeling I'd had back at the Family of Origin seminar after the vision of the child in white. Colour was gone again from the world, and I was once more standing on the edge of a precipice. Was I going to finally go over it, after all I'd been through?

I got in my car and mechanically drove home. I thought of my children. I thought of the pain and heartache of the years and wondered how I was going to cope with what I was feeling and the new knowledge I'd acquired. It seemed I would never feel sane, safe, able or normal, but continually fragmented and unreal. Any structure I had managed to build inside myself seemed to have vanished. With nothing to hold me up, I was again jelly in my own skin.

Once inside my home, I stood next to the telephone feeling the need to talk to somebody, anybody. I felt so alone. I thought of my mother but knew I couldn't call her. I'd rung after recovering the memory of choking on a penis, only to have her abruptly change the subject as soon as I alluded to struggling with something new from childhood. I thought of a friend or two, but felt embarrassed at again being needy and vulnerable. What was I going to do? Who was I going to lean on to prop me up?

Standing in timeless indecision, I felt a dawning recognition that my session with the counsellor had been another one of those situations where I was seeking the approval of another for my interpretation of myself and my own experiences. Throughout my life, I'd continuously given my power away. When it came to the crunch, I believed someone else always knew better than I did.

It was something I'd done with Suzie, and another counsellor shortly after her, a Christian social worker I'd hoped would advise and help me through the ending of my marriage. I'd done a lot of journal writing at the time, trying to sort out the scrambled confusion of my thoughts and feelings, but also exploring the wise, watchful part I'd connected with while working with Suzie. During one of my sessions with the Christian social worker I handed her my journals, asking her to read them and tell me if what I was writing was madness, or a real and sound aspect of myself I could trust. Believing she was the genuine, caring, Christian she proclaimed herself to be, I let her take them home to read.

However, it soon became obvious her primary agenda was money. She suddenly started charging extra even though she knew my tentative financial situation, and tried to charge me a large sum for a phone conversation we'd had outside our counselling sessions. There'd been no mention of a fee when she'd insisted I could ring anytime, assuring me she understood my situation and all she wanted to do was help. I chose not to continue, and she burnt my journals out of spite.

I was still doing the same thing, disowning important parts of myself and running to another for sanction of my sanity. Only this time, I'd been rudely and mercilessly forced back to myself, set up by Life to learn the lessons of self-acceptance and self-trust.

I became abruptly conscious of two aspects of myself trying to resolve the situation I was in now. I had an unexpected, almost out-of-body experience. From a higher perspective I could see clearly what I was doing, feel myself again as a wounded child in search of love, care and attention.

In that moment it was as if I travelled back through time, rapidly going over all I'd been through in the past, all the desperate ways I'd tried to get love, acknowledgement, resolution, and a sense of worthiness through the approval of others and the acceptance of my family.

I remembered the rejection of my parents and siblings when I first began to raise the issue of my buried childhood. The family closed ranks following a letter I'd written to my father, breaking my silence and imploring him to hear the truth of my painful childhood experiences, and the terror he himself had inflicted on me. All I wanted was for him to know and understand me, to love and accept me, but I'd been naïve and in no way equipped to deal with the response it generated. I was labelled crazy and a troublemaker.

I remembered my frenetic attempts to find understanding, belief, safety and love from the people in my life in an effort to heal the pain I was in, and saw only the familiar rigid walls of stone. I remembered the years of mental anguish, the ways in which I'd tried to twist myself into an acceptable shape for the approval of others, and the way it had slowly destroyed me.

I saw myself crying broken child tears, rolled up in the foetal position on the shower floor in my home during my marriage, and the times I'd savagely banged my head against the shower walls in an attempt to rid myself of the explosive pressure in my mind. I remembered the countless times I'd imagined putting a shotgun to my head and pulling the trigger, visualising my brain exploding in blessed release from the torment I lived with. I could not accept me if others did not. It was the only way I had of knowing if I was real.

As I saw it all, felt the pain of it, the loneliness, the sorrow and the separation, it suddenly occurred to me I'd already been down that road. I'd been the victim and it had nearly killed me. Did I really need to do it again? Did I want to do it again? The insight struck me dumb. I was aware of the wise part in me watching to see what I was going to do, and felt Life's attendance waiting to see if I was ready to move beyond my history. I was being confronted with a choice.

I began to laugh as a realisation hit me. No! I do not need to do that again, I do not want to do that again. I was not going back. In that moment, a powerful shift occurred. Gentle and comforting warmth began to spread outward from the centre of my chest, melting away the anguish and fear. For the first time in my life I had a sense of solidness, and a glimpse of my potential as an independent individual, capable of a self-directed life.

Chapter 13

REWRITING THE DANCE

Vince had been Life's response to the letter I'd penned asking the universe for the perfect man. He didn't arrive in the package I'd romanticised, but most certainly as what I needed in order to grow beyond where I was stuck.

Prior to his arrival I lived a muddled and unstructured life, and there was no adult leadership in my home. I'd well and truly given up and abandoned the responsibility. Instead, I spent a lot of time pining for something I thought I didn't have. I wanted someone else's life, an easier life, not my own.

I lived in vacillating limbo regarding who I was and what I was doing, and not putting consistent effort into working with my potential or solving my problems, but I talked about it a lot and talk is cheap.

Life was not going to let me get away with it.

Through Vince, I was pushed into facing what I was trying to run from. It wasn't until our drama had finally finished playing out, that I realised 'Trigger', the internet nickname he used, was in fact a herald for his purpose. My involvement with him literally triggered the wounding I most needed to heal. His purpose fulfilled, our entangled dance simply and naturally ended. The energy driving it dissolved and we never contacted each other again.

In the eight months we were together, I learnt many things, the hard way. Surface intellectual knowledge integrated into a much deeper level of comprehension. What had only been in my head, descended to my heart, and I got it.

I had to learn not to take on other peoples' problems as if they were my own. I am not personally responsible for the feelings and hardships of everyone who comes into my life; they are, just as I am responsible for mine.

I didn't have any healthy boundaries that distinguished me as a solid person, with my own standards, morals, beliefs and values. I shape-shifted and borrowed from others to fit in, gain approval, or get what I thought I needed to survive.

To really manage life effectively, especially when it comes to boundaries and intimate relationships, a person must have the ability to be fully themselves and to trust and act on their own instincts. That was something I'd always been unable to do. I'd been so badly damaged by my history, I was most often immobilised. Like a scared rabbit frozen stiff by the glare of oncoming headlights, I frequently couldn't move in any direction, not even to save myself from what I could see coming right at me.

I also learnt the limitations of what I am, and am not capable of, when it comes to trying to help another. I am not stronger than the jaws of somebody else's addiction and it was never my battle. While engrossed in someone else's fight, I was not fighting for me.

I had to take back my will from trying to control Vince's journey and let "Life" deal with him, just as "Life" had justly dealt with me. Healing, change and growth must be a personal choice made as an act of free will. It cannot be coerced, manipulated or forced. If someone is not right for you, you must have the courage to leave and remain alone. You don't get on a bus that is not yours, then try to change the direction in which it is going.

What I felt for Vince was never love. He was a representation of my father and through him; I was unconsciously attempting to resolve my deepest wounding. The injured child in me had been activated by similarities and had set about her driven need to be loved by her abuser.

I wanted my father to love, accept and approve of me. Without it I was unlovable, unworthy and unable to grow beyond my stunted and limited identity. He'd stolen my soul and I wanted it back.

The issue of love was something that needed to be resolved. My efforts to understand it constantly left me without a definition by which to recognise it. In my desperation to know how to feel it, to be able to have it and give it, I'd prayed many times, only to be continually shown all the ways I myself was not a loving person. Life is like that. So often it teaches us to recognise the good we seek, by first showing us the very things about ourselves that keep us from it. My greatest hindrance to knowing love, has come from not being able to love myself.

I'd thought about God, the messages of the man Jesus, other spiritual guides and teachers, and marvelled at how they loved. Was I supposed to be that perfect and unconditional with mine? If that was a requirement, why couldn't I achieve it? Not being able to be perfect, get our lives flowing with goodness, peace and safety after the demise of my marriage was a constant reminder of how undeserving I was. If I could only get everything right, maybe I would finally be worthy of the sanctuary and love I so desperately craved.

But I also looked to those same teachings to manipulate with the intention of trying to change someone else for my own gain, rather than to humbly work with them to have them change me. What I hadn't comprehended was the difference between the higher spiritual principle of unconditional Love, and the flawed, idealised romantic love that exists within the sphere of imperfect and complex human relationships.

In my emptiness, I tried to force romantic love to fill the gaping hole inside myself, not knowing the difference between toxic love and the kind of healthy love, whole, balanced people can share. Now I do. The latter seeks to enslave, while the other seeks to invite freedom.

It was a difficult period, but I needed to learn just what it was I truly valued, believed and wanted. I had to ask myself some tough questions. Was I forever going to regard myself as the walking wounded? Would I always allow myself to be defined by the beliefs, needs, and wants of others? Would I forever live in chaos and the struggle to know love, to be someone who could never have the kind of life she really wanted?

I was offered a final choice, to either live out my past in the present, or grow beyond it into the woman I have it in me to become.

In my time with Suzie, I'd slipped deeper and deeper into my darkness, that part of myself that believed I was irrevocably damaged. I had no safety net and no mirror to show me a reflection of my Light. I wanted to go towards it but I was always being steered from it. It worked only to prevent and prolong my healing.

Abandoning myself, giving my power away to other people, books or things, is equivalent to the abandonment and rejection I experienced as a child only, as an adult, I am the one inflicting the pain of desertion upon myself.

What I have needed from others was never their way of being and believing, but support to find and facilitate the growth of my own valid path. We are all unique. One size of anything does not fit all.

I now know what God/Life was trying to show me. I am worthy and worthwhile, regardless of my imperfections. One cannot be human and be anything but fallible. I have everything within me I need for this journey, a birthright I can trust if I would only allow myself to love and accept who I really am. At our core we are all infused with the Divine Light of Life.

Nothing of who we are dies or is ever truly lost from us. Whatever retreated in injurious circumstances can be reclaimed, healed and transformed. Our lives and hearts renewed, new things can and will be born.

I also know Life is trying, ever trying to guide and bring us all home to the fullness of our being. No one is left behind, no matter the wrongs or wound. Life never gives up, never walks away or dismisses anyone. Life knows every pain, the injuries and falsehoods we carry, and all the corners in which we try to hide. Life seeks only to bring us freedom. There is no need to be afraid.

Filled with symbolism, life is a wondrous journey, and if you can learn to read the symbols, follow the messages and signs in your life, they will bring you steadily forward. Trust you are being facilitated by Life. This means dropping the self-image of being a victim, something that took me a long time to learn.

Yes, I was a victim of terror and abuse as a child. Yes, I was brutalised and deeply wounded. But I couldn't truly begin to heal until I'd come far enough to realise Life was not my enemy. I'd become my enemy. I had taken on the negative beliefs, fears and distortions of my childhood experiences. Astray in my isolated world, I viewed all things through clouded vision.

Comprehending my role as victim and realising the continuing source of power behind it, was a major breakthrough. Even so, there is much more road ahead. Healing is a process that moves in stages and layers, and our growth as human beings, our becoming, is a life-long journey, regardless of our histories.

Toxic shame was one of the biggest culprits for keeping me locked in my perpetual cycle of self-denigration and self-abuse. Poisonous levels of guilt initially cast me into my prison, but it was lethal, all-consuming humiliation and shame that made sure I never got out. They worked together like hand and glove.

All human emotions have a positive and negative side, with a sliding scale in between. Healthy guilt is a necessary requirement for human growth and maturation. Its purpose is to let us know when we have transgressed. It works to correct, to reposition us toward the light and keep us on our right path. But when guilt becomes poisonous, like shame, it can and will destroy.

Many have had similar and far worse experiences to me. The depth of struggle and turmoil to regain the shattered and scattered pieces of one's soul, repair an often-splintered mind and broken heart, is a brave and Shamanic journey of profound and courageous proportions. I honour the valour of the crossing. It is an arduous task, one that sadly is all too often not understood by many of the professionals in the conventional mental health care field, or by family or friends. To me, this is a grave travesty.

My parents did the best they knew how to do when I was growing up. Both carried their respective unresolved childhoods on their backs and into their marriage, along with the burdens disappointments, expectations and teachings of their time. My father was a sick and tormented man. Growing up he suffered abuse not only at the hands of the Church, his parents and their histories, but also his own sexual conflicts and traumas. My mother was a victim of domestic violence, an oppressed woman trapped in her own nightmare, also with unhealed issues of childhood sexual abuse.

That doesn't in any way excuse what happened to me. Abuse and neglect of children is wrong, period, and as my story illustrates, it has profound, long lasting and far reaching repercussions. Yet I understand why it happened, and how it came to be. From this place of understanding I forgive my father for what he did and liberate myself from the chains of guilt, shame, and blame. I know only too well where his demons came from, how they came to be mine, and in turn, how that has flowed through to affect my own children.

The child in the well, huddled in the cold, damp darkness of the underground, was born of rejection and shame. She has been found and loved by me. I pray that one day my father will find his own lost, hurt and frightened child. He will not be free until he confronts and embraces himself with the light of truth, love and ultimately, forgiveness.

When I look back over the generations of my family, I can clearly see the recipe behind disaster. The cycle we pass on, the legacy of our histories, are crosses to be borne by the next generation. Whatever remains unhealed within us is a yoke passed on to our children. Like a creeping ghost, its energy floats hidden and unresolved from past time into the present, where, with unseen hands, it affects future lives.

In working to heal our histories and reconnect with our innate spark of Light, we have the power to halt the passing of the ghost. We can heal, and in doing so, make peace with the past, alter the present and protect the future. We can change the quality not only of our own lives, but also of those who come after us.

As I continue to grow forward and heal the wounds and patterns I have lived with, my authentic self comes ever more to the forefront to take her rightful place. I become more solid and grounded, more whole, capable and confident with each piece of my Self I reclaim.

Feelings of loss are still a part of my experience, though my moments of melancholy weaken as I strengthen and lengthen my moments of faith and joy. When sorrow does come upon me, I have learned to retreat and tend to myself. No one else can do that for me. In re-aligning with my centre, the core truth of who I am, I find Grace, healing, peace and stability.

Situations and lessons will continue to cross my path. No doubt I will have more struggles. My healing and unfolding is in forward motion. That is as it should be. Nothing stays the same. I am in process towards my own becoming, a spiritual journey that gets wider with understanding and wisdom the more I am open to being taught. It's all about expansion.

I know that when I hit a wall, I'm exactly where I need to be. It's indication something in my life needs my attention, or there are illusions in need of shattering, patterns to be broken. There are more parts of myself to reclaim. I'm constantly learning, evolving, moving, changing and refining my dance with Life.

The time has come for me to choose for myself who I am, and how to express that choice as I move through the rest of my life. My mind, my thoughts, my beliefs, my dreams and ambitions, belong to me, not my family nor any religion, social group, or country.

I free myself from the illusions of my forefathers and release the burden of false beliefs, those encumbrances that kept me from knowing and loving myself. I will not be paralysed by fear anymore.

I am more than my past, more than the identity they gave me, and much more than I ever dared dream I could be. My essence is made of Light and Love.

With the telling of this story, I close the door to victim-hood and stand ready to move forward. I go with a vastness of being I am eager to know and explore, though my history will never be forgotten. It is my legacy, ever my teacher, and has become my friend.

Like the Phoenix I rise from the ashes, re-born in my own skin. The sun is at my back, all manner of new and wonderful opportunities are before me, and I am okay.

Epilogue

In the time since this book was completed, my father lost his struggle with secondary cancer. His spiritual heart and physical body were ravaged by his own story and the silent burdens he carried. I sat unacknowledged by his bedside for the two days it took him to pass. I took the opportunity to whisper in his ear that I loved and forgave him. With my hand resting on his arm and my heart open, I prayed that as he left this world, he would be received into the welcoming arms of Love.

> "No longer do I cry unseen,
> unheard, my voiceless soul song
> to the moon's shadowed light.
> Now I sing my song with love to the world,
> for I have come into the light of day."

Lynette Chennell

Acknowledgements

This book would not have evolved beyond its shaky beginnings without the challenging, nurturing support and eagle eye of Eris MacDonald, manuscript assessor, mentor and friend. She took an untrained novice with a penchant for purple prose, and turned her into a more aware, mature writer. I have no doubt she was hand chosen by Life to shepherd this writing journey. I am truly grateful for everything she has taught me.

I would also like to thank the Thursday Night Writers group at The Katharine Susannah Prichard Writers Centre. They welcomed, encouraged and supported me to believe in myself.

And finally, I acknowledge and give thanks to the presence and power of God/Life. Your love for me has never wavered. You weave a mystery of great and profound proportions.

Lynette Chennell

www.ingramcontent.com/pod-product-compliance
Lightning Source LLC
Chambersburg PA
CBHW071907290426

44110CB00013B/1307